BEYOND BIRDIES

Helping Your Child Win at Golf
and at Life

Joseph DiChiara
PGA Professional

ISBN:

979-8-9941422-0-2

979-8-9941422-1-9

First Edition: 2025

Cover design & Interior design by: RH Publishing

Printed in the United States of America

Contents

To every parent who has stood on a driving range, wondering if they're doing this right.

To every child who has picked up a golf club with dreams and joy in their eyes.

And to my own children, who taught me that love always matters more than scores.

MISSION AND VISION

Every child who picks up a golf club deserves to experience joy, growth, and connection through the game. This book represents my commitment to making that possibility a reality for all families, regardless of their golf background or aspirations.

INTRODUCTION

Why Joy Matters More than Trophies

Picture two different driving ranges on a Saturday morning.

At the first one, seven-year-old Emma is in tears as her father corrects her grip for the tenth time. "No, not like that!" he says, repositioning her hands yet again. She's been hitting balls for an hour, each swing accompanied by technical instruction. Her shoulders slump. The spark that made her beg her father to bring her to the range has dimmed to nothing.

At the second range, eight-year-old Marcus is laughing as he tries to hit balls between two trees his grandmother has designated as "goal posts." When he succeeds, they both cheer. When he misses, she asks, "What do you think would help it go straighter?" He experiments with a few strategies, picks the best one, and tries again. An hour flies by, and he begs for "just five more minutes!"

Both children are learning to golf. But only one is learning to love it.

This book is about raising young golfers like Marcus—children who develop real skills while maintaining deep joy for the game. It's based on modern research in child development, motor learning, and sports psychology, combined with decades of observing what actually works in youth golf.

THE CRISIS IN YOUTH GOLF

Here's a sobering statistic: 70 percent of children who start golf quit by age thirteen. Not because they lack talent. Not because golf is too hard. They quit because adults have turned the game into a grind, play into pressure, and robbed the experience of any fun or joy.

Traditional youth golf instruction treats children like small adults, emphasizing:

- Perfect positions from the start
- Repetitive drilling
- Constant error correction
- Early specialization
- Comparison and competition

But children aren't miniature adults. Their brains work differently. Their bodies develop differently. Their motivations are different. When we ignore these differences, we create young golfers who might have pretty swings but have lost their love for the game.

A BETTER WAY FORWARD

This book presents a research-based approach to raising confident, skilled, and joyful young golfers. You'll learn:

- How children actually acquire motor skills (hint: it's not through repetition)

- Why fun accelerates learning rather than detracting from it
- How to create a practice that transfers to the course
- When competition helps and when it hurts
- How to be the parent your young golfer needs

Most importantly, you'll discover how to give your child a gift that lasts far beyond junior golf: a lifelong relationship with a game that teaches resilience, integrity, patience, and joy.

WHO THIS BOOK IS FOR

This book is for any parent who:

- Has a child interested in golf
- Wants to support without pressuring
- Values long-term development over short-term results
- Believes a fun childhood matters more than trophies
- Seeks research-based guidance, not opinion

Whether your child just picked up their first club or dreams of college golf, these principles apply. The goal isn't to create the next Tiger Woods—it's to raise a child who finds lifelong joy and growth through golf.

YOUR GUIDE FOR THE JOURNEY

Throughout this book, you'll find:

- Age-specific guidelines for development
- Practical games and activities
- Real family stories
- Warning signs to watch for

- Scripts for common situations
- Monthly and yearly planning templates

Each chapter includes action items you can implement immediately. But remember: perfection isn't the goal. Small changes, implemented consistently with love, create remarkable transformations.

A PERSONAL NOTE

As both a golf professional and a parent, I've seen the damage that well-intentioned but misguided approaches can cause. I've watched talented children in tears who end up quitting. I've seen families torn apart by pressure surrounding golf. I've witnessed the light go out in too many young eyes.

But I've also seen the magic that happens when we get it right. Children who can't wait to practice. Families bonded through shared golf adventures. Young people who handle life's challenges with the resilience they learned on the golf course. These success stories inspired this book.

THE CHOICE BEFORE YOU

You stand at a crossroads. Down one path lies the traditional approach—early specialization, technical obsession, constant comparison, and too often, burnout by age fifteen.

Down the other path lies the approach in this book—skill development through joy, progress through play, and a lifelong love of the game.

The choice you make will echo through your child's entire life. Choose wisely. Choose joy.

THE SEVEN COMMITMENTS OF POSITIVE GOLF PARENTS

Consider making these commitments:

1. **"I commit to prioritizing my child's joy over their scores."** This means celebrating a day of laughter over a low round, choosing fun over perfection, and remembering why they started playing.

2. **"I commit to supporting without steering."** This means providing resources while letting them choose direction, being their safety net not their GPS, and trusting their journey.

3. **"I commit to modeling the behavior I want to see."** This means handling your own golf frustrations well, showing that golf is fun despite imperfection, and demonstrating lifelong learning.

4. **"I commit to keeping golf in perspective."** This means golf enhances life but doesn't dominate it, family comes before tournaments, and childhood fun matters more than trophies.

5. **"I commit to unconditional love regardless of performance."** This means your affection doesn't vary with scores, bad rounds don't equal disappointment, and children are valued for who they are, not how they play.

6. **"I commit to seeking help when needed."** This means recognizing when you're too involved, finding mentors and support, and admitting when you don't know.

7. **"I commit to protecting their love of the game."** This means choosing long-term joy over short-term success, reducing pressure when needed, and ensuring golf remains a gift, not a burden.

PART I

UNDERSTANDING YOUR YOUNG GOLFER

CHAPTER 1

How Children Really Learn Golf

Sarah was seven years old when her father brought her to her first golf lesson. Like most well-meaning parents, he had visions of proper technique developing from the start. The instructor positioned Sarah's hands precisely, adjusted her stance to shoulder width, and began explaining the importance of keeping her left arm straight.

Twenty minutes later, Sarah was in tears. "I can't do it right!" she sobbed. Her natural joy of swinging a club and watching the ball fly had been replaced by frustration and the beginning of what could have become a lifelong aversion to golf.

This scene repeats itself on driving ranges worldwide every day. Well-intentioned parents and coaches, armed with traditional teaching methods, unknowingly sabotage children's natural learning abilities and strip the joy from the game.

This chapter will transform how you think about your child's golf development. You'll discover why traditional instruction fails, what science tells us about how children actually learn motor skills, and most importantly, what you can do differently starting today.

THE TRADITIONAL APPROACH THAT DOESN'T WORK

Traditional golf instruction was designed by adults, for adults, based on how adults think they learn. But children's brains function fundamentally differently. Watch any traditional junior lesson and you'll see:

- Complex technical instructions about positions
- Emphasis on "correct" form from the start
- Repetitive drilling of the same motion
- Constant error correction
- Comparison to an ideal model
- Serious, focused atmosphere

Now watch children learn naturally—whether riding a bike, playing catch, or hitting a golf ball when no one's instructing them:

- Experimentation and exploration
- Joy and laughter
- Variety and creativity
- Learning through games
- Self-discovery of solutions
- Play-based atmosphere

The disconnect is profound. We've taken a game and turned it into a joyless series of positions to memorize.

WHAT SCIENCE TELLS US ABOUT MOTOR LEARNING

In the last two decades, research in motor learning and neuroscience has revolutionized our understanding of how children acquire physical skills. Here are the key findings:

Discovery 1: Children Learn Movements, Not Positions

When a child learns to throw a ball, they don't think about elbow angles. They focus on the target and their body self-organizes to create an effective motion. This is called "implicit learning," and it's how humans are designed to acquire motor skills.

Skills learned implicitly (without conscious position awareness) are:

- More resistant to pressure
- Better retained over time
- More adaptable to different situations
- More enjoyable to perform

Discovery 2: Variety Beats Repetition

The old model says "practice makes perfect" through repetition. But research shows that practicing with constant variation produces better results. When children practice with variety they:

- Develop better adaptability
- Maintain engagement longer
- Discover personal solutions
- Transfer skills to the course better
- Enjoy practicing more

Discovery 3: External Focus Transforms Performance

Research consistently shows that focusing on movement effects (external focus) produces better results than focusing on body movements (internal focus). For example:

- Internal focus: "Turn your shoulders"
- External focus: "Swing the club around the corner"

The performance difference is immediate and dramatic—often 20-30 percent improvement just from changing the focus of attention.

UNDERSTANDING YOUR CHILD'S DEVELOPING BRAIN

To support your child effectively, you need to understand what's happening developmentally:

Ages 5-7: The Foundation Years
- **Brain**: Concrete thinking dominates, limited attention span (5-10 minutes)
- **Motor skills**: Basic coordination developing
- **Learning style**: Through imitation and play
- **Golf approach**: Maximum variety and fun, no technical instruction

Ages 8-10: The Golden Years of Motor Learning
- **Brain**: Peak neuroplasticity, improved attention (10-20 minutes)
- **Motor skills**: Coordination rapidly improving
- **Learning style**: Strong implicit learning ability
- **Golf approach**: Games, challenges, and movement patterns, avoid position instruction

Ages 11-13: The Transition Phase
- **Brain**: Abstract thinking emerging, social awareness increasing
- **Motor skills**: Growth spurts may disrupt coordination
- **Learning style**: Can handle more complexity
- **Golf approach**: Support through changes, maintain playfulness

Ages 14-18: The Refinement Years
- **Brain**: Adult-like cognitive abilities developing
- **Motor skills**: Approaching adult capabilities
- **Learning style**: Can process complex information
- **Golf approach**: More structure acceptable, maintain joy

THE HIDDEN DAMAGE OF EARLY SPECIALIZATION

The pressure to specialize early in golf is intense but misguided. Research on youth sport development shows that early specialization leads to:

- Higher injury rates
- Increased burnout
- Reduced adult performance
- Lower lifelong sport participation

Meanwhile, early diversification (playing multiple sports) produces:

- Better overall athleticism
- Enhanced creativity and adaptability
- Greater enjoyment and motivation
- Higher elite performance rates

The best golfers typically didn't specialize until their early teens. They played multiple sports, developed broad athletic skills, and maintained their love of movement and sport.

CRITICAL PARENT REMINDER

Your love must never fluctuate based on their golf performance.

As you begin this journey of developing your young golfer, establish this foundation: They need to know with absolute certainty that bad rounds don't diminish your affection, and good rounds don't increase it. You love WHO they are, not HOW they play. Every lesson in this book builds on this foundation. Without unconditional love, nothing else matters.

WHAT YOUR CHILD REALLY NEEDS

Your role isn't to be a swing coach. It's to be a facilitator of joy, protector of intrinsic motivation, and provider of opportunities. This means:

Being the Joy Guardian
- Celebrating effort over outcome
- Focusing on fun over form
- Allowing mistakes without comment
- Sharing excitement for successes
- Keeping perspective

Creating Learning Opportunities
- Taking them to different courses
- Playing games on the range
- Creating backyard challenges
- Finding practice partners
- Varying conditions

Modeling the Right Behavior
- Showing joy in your own golf
- Handling mistakes gracefully
- Focusing on process over score
- Demonstrating lifelong learning

THE POWER OF QUESTIONS

The language you use shapes your child's experience. Instead of giving instructions, ask questions that promote discovery:

- Instead of: "You lifted your head"
- Ask: "What did you notice about that shot?"
- Instead of: "Your grip is wrong"
- Ask: "How did that feel in your hands?"
- Instead of: "Watch how I do it"
- Ask: "What would happen if you tried something different?"

RED FLAGS: WHEN TRADITIONAL INSTRUCTION HAS TAKEN HOLD

Watch for these warning signs:

Physical Red Flags
- Mechanical, robotic movements
- Loss of natural rhythm
- Decreased power and distance
- Tension in face and body

Mental Red Flags
- Multiple swing thoughts
- Fear of making mistakes
- Constant self-criticism
- Focus on positions over targets

Emotional Red Flags
- Decreased enjoyment
- Anxiety about playing
- Frustration with "failure"
- Loss of playfulness

If you see these signs, it's time to return to fundamentals: joy, play, and natural learning.

CHAPTER 1 ACTION ITEMS

This week, try these experiments:

1. **The Silent Round**: Play 9 holes with your child without offering any technical advice. Only encouragement and questions are allowed.
2. **The Joy Audit**: Rate your child's joy level (1-10) during practice, play, and when talking about golf. If any score is below 7, adjustments are needed.
3. **The Language Check**: For one practice session, count how many times you mention body positions versus targets and achievements.
4. **The Play Session**: Replace one practice with pure play—games, challenges, fun. No instruction allowed.

- Children learn movements, not positions
- Variety creates better golfers than repetition
- External focus beats internal focus
- Joy accelerates learning
- Your role is facilitator, not instructor

Remember: Your child didn't fall in love with golf because of perfect positions. They fell in love with the feeling of striking a ball and watching it soar. Your job is to nurture that love while skills develop naturally.

CHAPTER 2

Your Child's Unique Development Journey

Ten-year-old Kai stood frozen over his ball, paralyzed by seven different swing thoughts. Meanwhile, his sister Maya, age eight, was creating her own game—seeing how many different sounds she could make with her swing. "How do you DO that?" Kai asked after Maya hit another solid shot with zero technical thoughts.

"I don't know," Maya shrugged. "I just look where I want it to go."

In that simple exchange lies a profound truth: every child learns differently. Maya wasn't lucky—she was using her natural learning style. Kai wasn't struggling because he lacked talent—he was overthinking.

This chapter will help you discover your child's unique learning profile and development pattern. You'll learn to work with their natural tendencies rather than against them, accelerating progress while maintaining joy.

BEYOND ONE-SIZE-FITS-ALL

The golf industry loves systems. "Follow these steps." "Master these positions." But children aren't manufactured products. They're unique individuals with distinct:

- Learning patterns
- Energy rhythms
- Motivational drivers
- Physical capabilities
- Social preferences

When we force children into rigid systems, we crush what makes them special. When we build learning around their uniqueness, we amplify their natural genius.

THE FIVE DIMENSIONS OF GOLF LEARNING

Instead of trying to force your child into a box, observe them across five key dimensions:

Dimension 1: Processing Speed

How quickly does your child convert new information into action?

The Quick Processor (Hummingbird)

- Tries immediately after seeing
- Gets frustrated with long explanations
- Thrives on variety
- Learns through action

The Steady Processor (Owl)

- Watches multiple times before trying
- Likes to understand "why"
- Prefers depth over breadth
- Learns through understanding

The Variable Processor (Dolphin)

- Speed depends on interest
- Alternates between quick and slow
- Responds to energy levels
- Learns through inspiration

Dimension 2: Information Preference

What type of information helps your child learn best?

The Outcome Learner

- Focuses on where the ball goes
- Key question: "Did it work?"
- Best feedback: Result-oriented

The Feel Learner

- Focuses on physical sensations
- Key question: "How did that feel?"
- Best feedback: Sensation-based

The Pattern Learner

- Focuses on cause and effect
- Key question: "Why did that happen?"
- Best feedback: Connections explained

Dimension 3: Social Learning Context

How does your child learn best in relation to others?

The Solo Explorer

- Thrives while working independently
- Needs self-directed time
- Benefits from personal challenges

The Social Learner

- Thrives with peers
- Needs interactive learning
- Benefits from group energy

The Mentor Seeker

- Thrives with one-on-one guidance
- Needs personal attention
- Benefits from trusted relationships

Dimension 4: Motivation Type

What drives your child to improve?

Intrinsic Innovator

- Motivated by personal discovery
- Turned off by external pressure
- Celebrates new solutions

Achievement Seeker

- Motivated by accomplishment
- Turned off by lack of goals
- Celebrates reaching milestones

Social Connector

- Motivated by relationships
- Turned off by isolation
- Celebrates shared experiences

Dimension 5: Energy Management

How does your child's energy affect their learning?

The Steady Burner

- Consistent energy throughout
- Can handle longer sessions
- Predictable peak times

The Sprinter

- Intense bursts of energy
- Needs frequent breaks
- Variable peak times

The Wave Rider

- Energy ebbs and flows
- Needs flexible structure
- Unpredictable patterns

DISCOVERING YOUR CHILD'S PROFILE

Learning profiles aren't determined through testing—they're discovered through observation. Here's a four-week discovery process:

Week 1: Natural Observation

Simply watch without intervening. Notice what they gravitate toward, how they create games, when they concentrate best, and what makes them light up.

Week 2: Gentle Experiments

Try different approaches:

- Monday: Visual learning (show without explaining)
- Tuesday: Verbal learning (explain the why)
- Wednesday: Feel-based learning (focus on sensations)

- Thursday: Game-based learning (all play)
- Friday: Child's choice

Note engagement levels and natural preferences.

Week 3: Pattern Recognition

Look for consistent themes in processing, energy, and social preferences. What conditions produce the best learning?

Week 4: Profile Integration

Combine observations into their unique learning fingerprint.

MATCHING PRACTICE TO PROFILE

Once you understand your child's profile, you can design practice that feels natural:

For the Quick Processor + Social Learner:

- Rapid-fire challenges with friends
- Quick rotation between activities
- Immediate recognition
- Competitive elements

For the Steady Processor + Solo Explorer:

- Self-directed exploration time
- Deep dives into single skills
- Personal experiment journal
- Private practice space

For the Variable Processor + Mentor Seeker:

- Flexible structure

- One-on-one guidance
- Energy-based pacing
- Collaborative exploration

COMMON PROFILE MISMATCHES

When practice doesn't match profile, problems arise:

Mismatch: Quick Processor in Slow Lesson

- Signs: Fidgeting, frustration, disconnection
- Solution: Increase pace, minimize explanation, maximize doing

Mismatch: Solo Explorer in Group Setting

- Signs: Withdrawal, decreased performance
- Solution: Build in alone time, honor their preference

Mismatch: Feel Learner with Position-Focused Coach

- Signs: Confusion, mechanical movements, lost rhythm
- Solution: Translate positions to feelings, find compatible instruction

AGE AND PROFILE EVOLUTION

Your child's learning profile will evolve:

Ages 5-7: Profile Emergence

- Preferences just appearing
- Highly variable day-to-day
- Need maximum flexibility

Ages 8-10: Profile Stabilization

- Patterns becoming clear
- Can articulate needs
- Preferences strengthening

Ages 11-13: Profile Complexity

- Multiple dimensions active
- Context-dependent shifts
- Self-awareness growing

Ages 14+: Profile Ownership

- Can self-advocate
- Understands own needs
- Drives own development

CHAPTER 2 ACTION ITEMS

This week, begin discovering your child's profile:

1. **Silent Observation**: Watch three practice sessions without intervening. Document natural patterns.
2. **The Experiment Week**: Try different approaches each day. Note which create the most engagement.
3. **The Learning Conversation**: Ask your child what makes practice fun, when they learn best, and what helps them remember.
4. **The Mismatch Audit**: Identify current practice elements that don't match your child's emerging profile.

REMEMBER: YOUR CHILD IS NOT BROKEN

The golf world wants every junior in the same box. But your child's unique learning profile is their superpower, not a problem to fix. When you honor how they learn best, you:

- Accelerate development
- Preserve joy
- Build confidence
- Strengthen your relationship
- Create sustainable success

There's no "best" learning profile. Quick processors aren't better than steady ones. Solo explorers aren't worse than social learners. Each profile has its path to golf excellence.

Your job isn't to change your child's profile. It's to help golf instruction adapt to their natural genius.

CHAPTER 3

Creating the Right Environment

The contrast at the junior tournament was striking. In one group, parents huddled together comparing their children's swings on video, discussing technical flaws, and planning intensive lesson schedules. Their children looked tense, checking constantly for parental approval after each shot.

In another group, families were laughing, playing card games between rounds, and talking about everything except golf. Their children seemed relaxed, chatting with competitors, and playing with visible joy despite the pressure.

Both groups had talented young golfers. But only one group was creating an environment where those golfers could thrive long-term.

This chapter explores how to create an environment—physical, emotional, and social—that nurtures confident, joyful young golfers. Because talent alone doesn't determine success. The environment you create does.

THE THREE ENVIRONMENTS THAT MATTER

1. The Physical Environment

Where and how your child practices shapes their relationship with golf.

At Home: Creating practice opportunities doesn't require a massive backyard or expensive equipment. Simple setups can provide hours of skill development:

- Putting areas using cups and obstacles
- Chipping zones with buckets or hula hoops as targets
- Safe hitting areas with foam balls
- Creative obstacles using household items

The key is making practice accessible and inviting, not perfect.

At Practice Facilities: How you use traditional facilities matters more than which ones you use:

- Claim creative spaces beyond the standard hitting bay
- Bring materials for games and challenges
- Use the entire facility creatively
- Find quieter times for relaxed practice
- Make it an adventure, not an obligation

On the Course: Transform course time from performance tests to learning laboratories:

- Play from appropriate distances
- Allow mulligans for learning
- Create games within the game
- Focus on experience over score
- Build positive memories

2. The Emotional Environment

The emotional climate you create determines whether golf becomes a source of joy or stress.

Characteristics of a Healthy Emotional Environment:

- Mistakes are learning opportunities
- Questions are encouraged
- Experimentation is rewarded
- Comparison is eliminated
- Fun is prioritized
- Effort matters more than outcome

Warning Signs of a Toxic Emotional Environment:

- Tension after bad shots
- Reluctance to try new things
- Concern about others watching
- Score obsession
- Practice avoidance
- Drop in creativity

Creating Emotional Safety: Your child needs to know that your love and approval don't depend on their golf performance. This means:

- Celebrating courage to try, not just successful outcomes
- Discussing the day's fun moments, not just scores
- Showing equal enthusiasm whether they play well or poorly
- Letting them see you enjoy playing golf despite imperfection
- Making golf one part of life, not life's center

3. The Social Environment

The people surrounding your young golfer profoundly impact their development.

Seek Out:

- Families who prioritize joy over results
- Instructors who understand child development
- Peer groups who support each other
- Facilities with positive youth culture
- Communities that celebrate all improvement levels

Avoid:

- Hypercompetitive parents living through their children
- Coaches focused solely on positions
- Negative peer groups that mock mistakes
- Facilities catering only to elite players
- Communities obsessed with rankings

THE POWER OF LANGUAGE

The words used in your golf environment shape your child's mindset:

Transform Your Family's Golf Vocabulary:

Instead of: "That was wrong" Say: "What did you learn from that shot?"

Instead of: "You need to practice more" Say: "When would you like to play next?"

Instead of: "Look at how well Sarah is doing" Say: "I love watching you discover your own stylc"

Instead of: "Don't mess up" Say: "Trust yourself and have fun"

CREATING RITUALS THAT SUPPORT GROWTH

Positive rituals build security and joy:

Pre-Round Rituals:

- Special breakfast together
- Playlist for the drive
- Gratitude practice
- High fives and hugs
- "Have fun" not "play well"

During-Round Support:

- Stay calm regardless of scores
- Focus on effort and attitude
- Provide snacks and hydration
- Offer encouragement, not advice
- Be present without hovering

Post-Round Rituals:

- Celebrate something specific and positive
- Share your favorite moment
- Get food before any golf discussion
- Let them decompress
- End with "I love to watch you play"

ENVIRONMENTAL DESIGN FOR DIFFERENT AGES

Ages 5-8: The Magic Years

- Maximum imagination in physical spaces
- Emotional environment of pure acceptance
- Social environment of play, not competition

Ages 9-12: The Growth Years

- Physical challenges that build skills
- Emotional support through struggles
- Positive peer relationships

Ages 13-16: The Identity Years

- Spaces for independent practice
- Emotional environment respecting autonomy
- Social connections with like-minded peers

Ages 17+: The Transition Years

- Professional-feeling physical environment
- Emotional support for major decisions
- Social networks supporting future goals

WHEN ENVIRONMENT NEEDS ADJUSTMENT

Watch for these signs that environmental changes are needed:

Physical Environment Red Flags:

- Child avoids practice spaces
- Boredom with current setup
- No creative play happening
- Injuries from poor setup

Emotional Environment Red Flags:

- Anxiety before golf
- Fear of disappointing you
- Lost joy in playing
- Pressure overwhelming fun

Social Environment Red Flags:

- Negative peer influences
- Comparison-based culture
- Adult drama affecting children
- Isolation from golf friends

CREATING YOUR ENVIRONMENTAL ACTION PLAN

This week, assess and improve each environment:

Physical Environment Audit:

- List current practice spaces
- Identify one improvement for each
- Add one creative element
- Remove one source of stress

Emotional Environment Check:

- Monitor your reactions to good/bad shots
- Count positive vs. corrective comments
- Note your child's emotional state
- Adjust your approach accordingly

Social Environment Evaluation:

- List golf-related social connections
- Identify positive and negative influences
- Seek one new positive connection
- Distance from one negative influence

THE ENVIRONMENT SUCCESS STORY

The Martinez family transformed their golf environment with simple changes:

- Converted their garage into a fun practice space with targets and games
- Instituted "Taco Tuesday" after practice
- Found three families with similar joy-first values
- Changed instructors to one who emphasized play
- Created a "wall of fun" with golf photos and memories

Result: Their daughter went from wanting to quit to begging for more practice time. Her scores improved as a bonus, but more importantly, her love for golf was restored.

CHAPTER 3 ACTION ITEMS

- Environment shapes development more than talent
- Physical spaces should invite creative practice
- Emotional climate must prioritize joy and growth
- Social connections can support or sabotage
- Small environmental changes create big results
- Your ability to influence the environment is your superpower

Remember: You can't control your child's talent, but you can completely control the environment where they learn, practice, and develop skills. Make it one where confidence blooms, joy flourishes, and a lifelong love of golf takes root.

CHAPTER 4

The Parent's Role in Youth Golf

During Emma's Tuesday evening lesson, her mother received a text from the instructor: "Can you pick Emma up early? I need to talk with you."

When her mother arrived, she found nine-year-old Emma in tears and the instructor looking frustrated. "She's not following my instructions," he explained. "I keep telling her the correct positions, but she won't focus. Maybe you could work with her at home on what I'm teaching?"

Emma's mother faced a defining moment. She could side with the instructor, adding her voice to the chorus of criticism. Or she could recognize that something was fundamentally wrong with this picture—her joyful, eager daughter transformed into a sobbing child who now said she hated golf.

She chose wisely. "Emma and I are going to take a break and reassess," she said calmly. "Thank you for your time."

That night began a transformation in how Emma's family approached golf. They discovered that the most crucial factor in Emma's development wasn't finding the perfect instructor or program—it was understanding their role as parents in her golf journey.

THE PARENT PARADOX

Being a golf parent presents unique challenges. You want to support without smothering, encourage without pressuring, and help without hovering. You're investing time and money while trying not to become invested in outcomes. You're navigating a sport with individual performance but social dynamics, technical complexity but the need for simplicity.

Most challenging of all: you're trying to give your child wings while keeping them grounded.

THE FIVE PARENT TYPES (AND WHY BALANCE MATTERS)

I've noticed golf parents tend to fall into the following five categories. Becoming aware of your patterns and behaviors can help you provide the support your child actually needs:

1. The Technical Director
- Constantly offers swing advice
- Films every shot for analysis
- Speaks in golf terminology
- Focuses on positions over play

The Problem: Creates mechanical, self-conscious golfers who lose natural athleticism and joy.

The Balance: Channel technical interest into creating fun challenges instead of position fixes.

2. The Achievement Manager
- Tracks every statistic
- Constantly compares them to other juniors
- Plans tournament schedule years ahead
- Measures worth through results

The Problem: Builds pressure that crushes intrinsic motivation and creates fear of failure.

The Balance: Celebrate process goals and personal growth over competitive outcomes.

3. The Helicopter Caddie
- Hovers during practice
- Intervenes at every struggle
- Makes all decisions
- Protects their child from all failure

The Problem: Prevents development of independence, resilience, and problem-solving skills.

The Balance: Be available but give them space; let them own their journey.

4. The Hands-Off Observer
- Drops off and disappears
- Shows little interest
- Provides no emotional support
- Misses important moments

The Problem: The child feels unsupported and questions if their efforts matter.

The Balance: Show genuine interest while respecting their space and autonomy.

5. The Balanced Supporter

- Provides resources without pressure
- Celebrates effort and improvement
- Allows ownership of the journey
- Maintains perspective on golf's role

The Goal: This is where all parents should aim to be, adjusting their approach based on the child's needs.

YOUR EVOLVING ROLE THROUGH THE YEARS

Your role must adapt as your child develops:

Ages 5-8: The Playmate

- Primary role: Make golf fun
- Join in games and activities
- Create joyful associations
- No technical input needed
- Protection from pressure is essential

Key actions:

- Play alongside them
- Invent silly games
- Celebrate everything
- Ignore "mistakes"
- Build pure joy

Ages 9-12: The Facilitator

- Primary role: Provide opportunities
- Arrange practice and play
- Find appropriate instruction
- Build social connections
- Support emerging independence

Key actions:

- Ask what they want
- Provide options
- Connect with families
- Support their choices
- Step back gradually

Ages 13-16: The Consultant

- Primary role: Support their vision
- Respond to requests
- Provide resources
- Emotional stability
- Respect autonomy

Key actions:

- Listen more than speak
- Offer when asked
- Respect decisions
- Maintain perspective
- Trust their process

Ages 17+: The Advisor

- Primary role: Trusted counsel
- Available when needed
- Wisdom without interference
- Life balance perspective
- Transition support

Key actions:

- Wait to be asked
- Share experience carefully
- Support all paths
- Celebrate maturity
- Maintain connection

PRACTICAL STRATEGIES FOR COMMON SITUATIONS

When They Want to Quit:

- Listen without judgment
- Explore the real reason
- Offer a break, not an ultimatum
- Remove pressure immediately
- Let them lead the decision

When They're Not Improving:

- Check your definition of "improvement"
- Look beyond scores
- Celebrate other growth
- Reduce comparison
- Trust development timing

When Others Are "Better":

- Reinforce individual journey
- Highlight their unique strengths
- Avoid comparison conversations
- Find different peer groups
- Focus on personal progress

When They're Nervous:

- Normalize the feelings
- Share your own nervousness
- Focus on process, not outcome
- Reduce importance of event
- Ensure fun elements remain

When They Succeed:

- Celebrate effort first
- Keep success in perspective

- Share joy without adding pressure
- Let them own the moment
- Maintain same support level

THE POWER OF YOUR PRESENCE

Research shows that HOW you watch matters more than how often:

Positive Presence Looks Like:

- Calm body language
- Smiles and encouragement
- Attention without intensity
- Enjoyment of the experience
- Pride in effort, not just outcome

Negative Presence Includes:

- Tense positioning
- Constant coaching gestures
- Visible frustration
- Phone distraction
- Result-focused reactions

Your child reads your energy more than your words. They know if you're truly enjoying watching them or just enduring until they "get better."

UNCONDITIONAL LOVE: THE NON-NEGOTIABLE FOUNDATION

The most damaging thing you can do to your young golfer—worse than any technical mistake, worse than any missed tournament, worse than any wrong equipment—is to tie your love to their performance. Yet it happens subtly in countless families, creating wounds that last decades.

How Conditional Love Appears in Golf

It often starts innocently:

- Extra hugs and excitement after good rounds
- Quiet car rides after poor performance
- Detailed discussions about good shots, silence about bad ones
- Restaurant celebrations for low scores, straight home after high ones
- More affection during winning streaks
- Emotional distance during slumps

Children are emotional detectives. They notice everything:

- Your body language walking off 18
- The tone of your "good job"
- How long you wait before speaking
- Whether you make eye contact
- If your smile reaches your eyes
- How quickly you check your phone

What Children Conclude:

- "Mom is happier when I play well"
- "Dad loves me more when I win"
- "I'm valuable when I score low"
- "Bad golf makes me a bad person"
- "I must earn love through performance"

The Long-Term Damage

Children who experience conditional love through sports develop:

- **Performance-based self-worth**: Only feeling valuable when succeeding
- **Chronic anxiety**: Constant fear of losing love through failure
- **Perfectionism**: Desperate attempts to maintain affection
- **Emotional numbness**: Shutting down to avoid disappointment

- **Relationship problems**: Expecting all love to be earned
- **Identity confusion**: Not knowing who they are beyond achievements

Sarah's Story: "I'm thirty-four now, successful in my career, but I still hear my dad's silence after bad rounds. I catch myself working eighty-hour weeks trying to earn the love I should have received freely. Golf taught me that love must be earned, and I'm still unlearning that lie."

Building Unconditional Love Habits

The 24-Hour Rule: Your demeanor, affection, and treatment must be identical whether your child just:

- Won their first tournament or finished last
- Shot their best score or worst score
- Made clutch putts or missed from two feet
- Played courageously or fearfully

Practical Strategies:

1. The Consistent Greeting Create a post-round ritual that never varies:

- Same hug duration
- Same greeting words
- Same energy level
- Same next activity

Example: "There's my favorite golfer! Ready for our post-round smoothie?"

2. The Love Reminder Regularly reinforce unconditional love:

- "I love watching you play, no matter what happens"
- "You know what makes me proud? That you're my child"
- "Win or lose, you're coming home to the same amount of love"

- "Your score will be forgotten tomorrow, but you'll still be my favorite person"

3. The Mood Check Before reacting to any round:

- Take three deep breaths
- Remember your child's age
- Choose love over analysis
- Save teaching for later
- Focus on connection first

4. The Bad Round Response When they play poorly and expect your disappointment:

- "I'm proud of your effort and not giving up"
- "What was fun today?"
- "I love you exactly the same"
- "Want to do something fun together?"
- Physical affection without words

5. The Good Round Response

When they play well and seek extra validation:

- Give the same energy as bad rounds
- Celebrate their joy, not the score
- "You seemed to enjoy that!"
- "Your smile made my day"
- Avoid score-based praise

Red Flags You're Sending Conditional Love Signals

Child's Behaviors:

- Apologizing for bad scores
- Hiding scorecards
- Emotional breakdowns in anticipation of your reaction
- Saying "I played terrible, I'm sorry"
- Checking your face before sharing results

- Playing tight when you're watching

Your Behaviors:

- Different car ride energy based on scores
- Calling relatives only after good rounds
- Posting social media only about wins
- Detailed discussion of good rounds, quick dismissal of bad ones
- Physical distance after poor play
- Using golf performance in discipline ("You can't focus in golf or homework!")

If you recognize these patterns, immediately:

- Apologize to your child
- Explicitly state your love is constant
- Modify your behaviors
- Seek professional help if needed
- Monitor your reactions vigilantly

The Ultimate Test

Ask yourself honestly:

- Would I treat my child differently if they never played golf again?
- Do I light up the same way seeing them at breakfast as I do after a birdie?
- Is my love as visible after a 95 as after a 75?
- Would they feel equally loved if they quit tomorrow?

If you hesitated on any answer, work is needed.

Creating Unconditional Love Statements

Replace performance-based language:

1. "I'm so proud you won!" "I'm so proud of your effort!"

2. "Great round! You made me happy!" "I love seeing you happy!"
3. "That was disappointing" "How are you feeling about it?"
4. "You'll get them next time" "I enjoyed watching you today"
5. "Why did you make that decision?" "Tell me about your thought process"

The Family Meeting Solution

Hold a family meeting specifically about unconditional love:

- **Parent Statement**: "We need to make something crystal clear. Our love for you has nothing to do with golf. You could quit tomorrow, never touch a club again, and receive exactly the same amount of love."
- **Child Response**: Let them share any times they felt love was conditional
- **Apologies**: If patterns existed, genuinely apologize
- **New Commitment**: Create family rules about showing consistent love
- **Regular Check-ins**: Monthly ask: "Have you felt my love change based on golf?"

CREATING FAMILY GOLF VALUES

Develop clear family values around golf:

Example of Family Golf Values:

- Fun comes first, always
- Effort matters more than outcome
- Everyone develops differently
- Golf brings us together
- Mistakes are how we learn
- Character trumps scores

Post these visibly. Reference them often. Live them consistently.

WHEN YOU'RE GETTING IT RIGHT

Signs you're fulfilling your role well:

- Your child asks to practice
- They share golf experiences eagerly
- They handle setbacks resiliently
- They own their improvement
- They play with joy
- They thank you for support
- Golf strengthens your relationship

Signs you need to adjust:

- Golf creates family tension
- Your child seems anxious
- They hide scores or struggles
- Practice becomes a battle
- Joy is disappearing
- They play for you, not themselves
- Golf divides your relationship

CHAPTER 4 ACTION ITEMS

This week, strengthen your role as a positive golf parent:

- **Role Assessment**: Identify which parent type you most resemble. Choose one behavior to increase and one to decrease.
- **Commitment Ceremony**: Review the seven commitments with your family. Sign them together and post them visibly.
- **Presence Practice**: During the next practice or round, focus entirely on being positively present. Notice your child's response.
- **Values Creation**: Work with your child to create 3-5 family golf values. Make it collaborative and fun.

THE ULTIMATE PARENT SCORECARD

Your success as a golf parent isn't measured by your child's handicap or tournament wins. It's measured by:

- Do they love playing?
- Are they developing resilience?
- Is golf bringing you closer?
- Are they learning life lessons?
- Will they play as adults?
- Do they own their journey?
- Are they thriving in all areas?

If you can answer "yes" to these questions, you're winning the only game that matters.

REMEMBER YOUR WHY

In the challenging moments—and there will be many—remember why you introduced your child to golf. Not to create a professional. Not to win a college scholarship. But to give them:

- A lifelong sport
- Lessons in perseverance
- Time together
- Healthy challenges
- Social connections
- Joy in movement
- Tools for life

Your role is to protect and nurture these gifts, and prevent competition from corrupting them.

Emma's mother understood this. Six months after leaving that tearful lesson, Emma was back on the course—playing with friends, creating her own games, and begging to practice. Her mother's role had evolved from trying to enforce someone else's system to protecting her daughter's love of the game.

That's your role too. To nurture a child who happens to play golf—and plays it with joy.

PART II

BUILDING SKILLS THROUGH PLAY

CHAPTER 5

Making Practice Fun and Effective

Saturday morning at the driving range revealed two completely different worlds. On one end, seven-year-old Stephen hit ball after ball with his 7-iron while his father counted: "That's forty-seven... forty-eight... forty-nine... Just one more to make fifty!" Stephen's shoulders slumped, his swings becoming increasingly mechanical, his expression blank.

On the other end, nine-year-old Sofia was laughing as she played "Golf Battleship" with her grandmother. They'd set up targets at different distances, calling out coordinates and trying to "sink" each other's ships with precise shots. "B-4!" Sofia announced, grabbing a different club. "I'm going to curve this one around your destroyer!"

An hour later, Stephen was begging to leave while Sofia pleaded for "just five more minutes!" Both children had practiced. Only one had learned—and loved it.

This chapter will transform how you think about practice. You'll discover why traditional repetitive practice fails young golfers, learn dozens of games that build real skills, and most importantly, understand how to make practice so engaging your child begs for more.

THE PRACTICE REVOLUTION

Everything you've been told about practice is probably wrong. The old model—repetition builds skill—comes from factory thinking: repeat the same motion enough times and it becomes automatic. But children aren't machines, and golf isn't an assembly line.

Why Traditional Practice Fails:

- **The Boredom Factor**: Young brains crave novelty. Repetition without variation literally shuts down learning centers in the brain.
- **The Transfer Problem**: Skills learned through blocked practice (same shot repeatedly) don't transfer to the course where every shot is different.
- **The Joy Destroyer**: Nothing kills love for an activity faster than turning play into work.
- **The Creativity Killer**: Repetitive practice eliminates problem-solving and discovery—the very things that create adaptable golfers.

THE SCIENCE OF EFFECTIVE PRACTICE

Research shows that effective practice for young golfers must include:

- **Variability**: Constantly changing conditions improves learning and retention
- **Challenge**: Appropriate difficulty (not too easy, not too hard) maximizes engagement
- **Autonomy**: Allowing choice and ownership accelerates development
- **Purpose**: Understanding "why" creates deeper learning
- **Fun**: Positive emotions enhance neuroplasticity and memory formation

AGE-APPROPRIATE PRACTICE DESIGN

Ages 5-7: The Magic Years (20-30 minutes maximum)

At this age, practice is 100 percent play:

Session Structure:

- 5 minutes: Free exploration with equipment
- 20 minutes: 3-4 different games (5-7 minutes each)
- 5 minutes: Child's choice activity

Game Examples:

- **Animal Golf**: Hit shots like different animals (mouse = soft, elephant = powerful)
- **Rainbow Targets**: Colorful targets at varying distances, paint rainbows with ball flights
- **Pirate Treasure**: Collect treasure by hitting balls to specific areas
- **Magic Wands**: Clubs become wands casting spells on golf balls

Key Principles:

- Story drives everything
- Success is broadly defined
- Constant variety
- No position focus
- End when energy drops

Ages 8-10: The Skill Discovery Years (30-45 minutes)

Practice becomes structured play:

Session Structure:

- 5 minutes: Dynamic warm-up game
- 30 minutes: 4-5 skill games with variety
- 5 minutes: Cooldown challenge
- 5 minutes: Reflection and celebration

Game Examples:

- **Distance Detective**: Set up cones or obstacles at a variety of distances, guess and test with different clubs
- **Shape Master**: Draw cards to determine required shot shape
- **Pressure Ladder**: Progressive challenges with increasing difficulty
- **Golf Olympics**: Multiple events testing different skills

Key Principles:

- Games teach skills
- Mild pressure introduced
- Choices offered
- Progress tracked playfully
- Social elements included

Ages 11-13: The Competitive Awakening (45-60 minutes)

Practice blends play with purpose:

Session Structure:

- 10 minutes: Skill-specific warm-up
- 20 minutes: Focused skill development through games
- 20 minutes: Course simulation or pressure training
- 10 minutes: Cooldown and planning

Game Examples:

- **9-Shot Challenge**: Create matrix of trajectories and shapes
- **Course Architect**: Design and play holes on range

- **Pressure Pyramid**: Stakes increase with each success
- **Random Golf**: App generates random shot requirements

Key Principles:

- Purpose explained
- Competition integrated
- Transfer emphasized
- Ownership building
- Fun is still central

Ages 14+: The Performance Years (60-90 minutes)

Practice becomes sophisticated but maintains engagement:

Session Structure:

- 15 minutes: Professional warm-up
- 30 minutes: Deliberate practice with variety
- 30 minutes: Transfer and pressure work
- 15 minutes: Recovery and reflection

Game Examples:

- **Tournament Simulation**: Full pre-round routines and pressure
- **Skills Circuit**: Rotating stations with specific challenges
- **Win or Go Home**: Elimination format building pressure
- **Create and Teach**: Design drills to teach others

Key Principles:

- Athlete-led design
- Performance focus
- Transfer priority
- Mental training integrated
- Joy protected

PRACTICE GAME LIBRARY

Full Swing Games

1. Target Roulette

- Setup: 5+ targets visible
- Game: Spin wheel or draw cards for target selection
- Skills: Adaptability, distance control
- Variations: Add shape requirements, time pressure

2. 21 (Golf Version)

- Setup: Assign point values to different targets
- Game: First to reach exactly 21 wins (go over = back to 11)
- Skills: Strategy, pressure, distance control
- Variations: Subtract points for misses

3. Shot Shape Art

- Setup: Obstacles create required shapes
- Game: Draw pictures with ball flights
- Skills: Trajectory control, creativity
- Variations: Partner draws, you create

4. The Elimination Game

- Setup: Start with all clubs
- Game: Bad shot = lose that club
- Skills: Adaptability, focus
- Variations: Time limits, specific targets

Short Game Games

5. Chipping Tic-Tac-Toe

- Setup: 9-square grid around green
- Game: Land in square to claim it
- Skills: Accuracy, strategy

- Variations: Different lies, must call square first

6. Up and Down Challenge

- Setup: Various positions around green
- Game: Complete circuit in fewest shots
- Skills: All short game shots
- Variations: Worst ball, time pressure

7. The Landing Zone

- Setup: Hula hoops or circles on green
- Game: Points for landing in zones
- Skills: Distance control, trajectory
- Variations: Moving zones, blind shots

Putting Games

8. Pressure Ladder

- Setup: Putts at 3, 6, 9, 12, and 15 feet
- Game: Make each to advance, miss = start over
- Skills: Pressure handling, consistency
- Variations: Must call speed, add break

9. Around the World

- Setup: 8 positions around hole
- Game: Make from each position
- Skills: Reading break, adaptability
- Variations: Time limit, match play

10. Speed Control Challenge

- Setup: Multiple distances, past hole target
- Game: Stop ball in scoring zone past hole
- Skills: Distance control, green reading
- Variations: Uphill/downhill, team format

MAKING PRACTICE IRRESISTIBLE

The Five Ingredients of Addictive Practice:

- **Autonomy**: Let them choose games, create rules, design challenges
- **Mastery**: Progress visible but new challenges ahead
- **Purpose**: They understand why each game builds skills
- **Social**: Involve friends, family, or imaginary competitors
- **Novel**: Something new or different each session

Environmental Design:

- Bring colorful equipment and props
- Create "stations" even in small spaces
- Use music for energy management
- Display progress visually
- Make setup/cleanup part of the fun

Energy Management:

- Start with their highest energy activity
- Alternate high/low intensity
- Include water and snack breaks
- End before exhaustion
- Always finish on a high note

COMMON PRACTICE PITFALLS TO AVOID

Pitfall 1: The Marathon Session

- Problem: Sessions are too long for attention span
- Solution: Multiple short sessions beat one long one
- Remember: End wanting more

Pitfall 2: The Perfection Trap

- Problem: Focusing on ideal technique over exploration
- Solution: Celebrate creativity and effort

- Remember: Function over form

Pitfall 3: The Comparison Game

- Problem: Measuring against other children
- Solution: Track personal progress only
- Remember: Individual journey

Pitfall 4: The Boredom Creep

- Problem: Same activities repeatedly
- Solution: Constant variety and evolution
- Remember: Novelty drives learning

CREATING YOUR PRACTICE PLANNING SYSTEM

Weekly Planning Template:

Monday: Skill Focus Day

- Choose one primary skill
- 3-4 games targeting that skill
- Progress measurement

Wednesday: Variety Day

- Multiple skills
- Quick rotations
- High energy

Friday: Fun Day

- Child chooses activities
- New games introduced
- Pure play

Weekend: Applied Learning

- Course play
- Practice with golf game elements
- Transfer focus

Keep Simple Records in a Practice Journal:

- Games played
- Child's favorites
- Progress noted
- Energy levels
- Ideas for next time

TECHNOLOGY AND PRACTICE

Use technology to enhance, not dominate:

Helpful Uses:

- Random club/target generators
- Simple game scoring apps
- Progress celebration videos
- Sharing achievements with family

Harmful Uses:

- Constant swing analysis
- Comparison to others
- Position obsession
- Replacing human interaction

CHAPTER 5 ACTION ITEMS

This week, revolutionize your practice approach:

- **The Game Creation Session**: Spend 30 minutes with your

child creating three new practice games. Let them lead design.
- **The Variety Audit**: List your last five practice activities. If any are repeated, add five new games to your repertoire.
- **The Energy Experiment**: Try the same game at different times/days. Note when your child engages most.
- **The Joy Measurement**: Rate fun level (1-10) for each practice this week. Adjust until scores are consistently above eight.

SIGNS OF PRACTICE SUCCESS

You know practice is working when:

- Your child asks to go
- They create their own games
- Time flies during sessions
- They want to show others what they learned
- Bad shots don't ruin mood
- They practice without you asking
- Golf becomes their idea

THE LONG-TERM VIEW

Effective practice isn't about perfecting positions today. It's about:

- Building a love for improvement
- Developing problem-solving skills
- Creating positive associations
- Establishing lifelong habits
- Fostering creativity
- Building resilience
- Maintaining joy

Every practice session writes a small chapter in your child's golf story. Make sure those chapters are filled with discovery, laughter, and growth—not tedium, frustration, and pressure.

YOUR PRACTICE TRANSFORMATION STARTS NOW

Tomorrow, instead of heading to the range with a bucket of balls and vague plans for "getting better," arrive with games, props, and enthusiasm. Watch your child's eyes light up. See them engage completely. Notice skills developing naturally through play.

Because when practice becomes play, learning becomes inevitable, and golf becomes a joyful sport that lasts a lifetime.

Remember Stephen from the beginning of the book? His father implemented games from this chapter and transformed their sessions. Last week, Stephen created his own practice game involving superheroes and challenged his dad to play. They laughed for an hour, and Stephen hit the best shots of his young life.

That type of transformation is waiting for your family too. It starts with your next practice session.

What game will you play tomorrow?

Chapter 6

Developing Feel over Mechanics

The junior golf clinic was in full swing when eight year old Mia raised her hand. "Coach, I found something! When I pretend I'm painting a rainbow with my club, the ball goes really high and soft!"

The instructor frowned. "That's nice, Mia, but let's focus on the proper technique. You need to shift your weight to your left side, maintain your spine angle, and release the club at impact while keeping your head..."

Mia's eyes glazed over. While attempting to remember all those positions, her next shot skulled across the green. The "rainbow painter" was gone, replaced by a mechanical, confused child who would spend the next two years trying to recapture the natural feel she'd discovered and lost in that moment.

Meanwhile, on the putting green, ten-year-old James was having a breakthrough. His grandfather had asked him a simple question: "If you were rolling this ball to me with your hand, how hard would you roll it?" James made the motion, then replicated that feel with his putter. The ball rolled perfectly to the hole. "That's it!" James exclaimed. "It feels like tossing it!"

Two children. Two approaches. Two completely different futures in golf.

This chapter will show you how to develop your child's natural feel for the game—the internal sense that creates fluid, athletic golfers rather than mechanical robots. You'll learn why feel matters more than positions, how to cultivate it, and most importantly, how to protect it from well-meaning destruction.

THE FEEL REVOLUTION

Golf instruction has it backward. For generations, we've tried to build golf swings from the outside in—positions first, hoping feel will follow. But watch any great athlete in any sport. They don't think about positions. They feel their way to excellence.

What Is Feel? Feel is your child's internal sense of:

- How hard to hit for different distances
- Where the clubface is pointing
- The rhythm that produces solid contact
- How to adjust for different conditions
- The difference between tension and flow

Feel is wisdom the body possesses that the mind cannot fully articulate. It's what allows a child to adjust their bike balance without thinking, throw a ball to different distances naturally, or know exactly how hard to kick a soccer ball to a teammate.

WHY FEEL BEATS MECHANICS

The Performance Paradox

Studies of athletes under pressure reveal a stunning truth: the more they think about technique, the worse they perform. Why? Because conscious control interferes with the subconscious systems that actually produce skilled movement.

When your child focuses on feel:

- Movement remains fluid and natural
- Adjustments happen automatically
- Pressure doesn't disrupt performance
- Joy and flow states are possible
- Individual style emerges

When they focus on positions:

- Movement becomes robotic
- Adjustment requires conscious thought
- Pressure causes technique breakdown
- Anxiety replaces joy
- Cookie-cutter swings develop

THE DEVELOPMENT OF FEEL

Feel develops through exploration, not instruction. Here's how it emerges at different ages:

Ages 5-7: Pure Feel

Young children are feel machines. They haven't yet developed the cognitive capacity for complex position awareness, so they naturally rely on feel. This is why a six year old can often putt better than adults—they just look and react.

Protecting feel at this age:

- Never mention positions
- Encourage their descriptions ("It feels swooshy!")
- Use their language in your response to them
- Celebrate their discoveries
- Keep everything external ("Hit it over the tree" not "Turn your shoulders")

Ages 8-10: Feel Under Threat

This is when well-meaning adults often begin destroying feel with technical instruction. Children's growing cognitive abilities make them capable of thinking about positions, but doing so sabotages their natural athleticism.

Developing feel at this age:

- Ask "How did that feel?" constantly
- Encourage experimentation
- Use analogies and images
- Create feel challenges
- Resist technical language

Ages 11-13: Feel vs. Mechanics Battle

Adolescents face pressure to look "correct" and often abandon feel for positions. This is when many natural athletes become mechanical golfers.

Preserving feel at this age:

- Validate their natural style
- Show examples of unique swings that work
- Focus on results, not appearance
- Build feel vocabulary
- Create safe spaces for experimentation

Ages 14+: Feel Integration

Older juniors can begin integrating some technical knowledge with feel, but feel must remain primary.

Advanced feel development:

- Sophisticated feel awareness
- Keep feel primary, introduce technical knowledge
- Feel-based adjustments
- Personal style confidence
- Teaching feel to others

BUILDING FEEL THROUGH GAMES AND ACTIVITIES

Distance Control Feel Games

1. The Toss Game

- First toss a ball to various targets
- Then hit to same targets
- Connect throwing feel to hitting feel
- "Make your swing feel like your toss"

2. Eyes Closed Challenge

- Hit shots with eyes closed
- Guess how far it went
- Builds internal distance calibration
- Removes visual interference

3. The Percentage Game

- Hit at 25 percent, 50 percent, 75 percent, 100 percent power
- Feel the differences
- No measurement initially, just feel
- Verify later with results

Touch and Trajectory Feel Games

4. The Height Controller

- Create shots of different heights
- Use feel words: "floaty," "punchy," "skimmer"
- No technical instruction
- Celebrate variety

5. The Bounce Predictor

- Before chipping, predict bounces
- Adjust feel to achieve prediction
- Builds cause-effect awareness
- Feel becomes purposeful

6. The Sound Game

- Different shots make different sounds
- "Make a click," "Make a thud," "Make a swoosh"
- Sound indicates quality
- Feel produces sound

Rhythm and Tempo Feel Games

7. The Music Matcher

- Swing to different song tempos
- Feel rhythm in whole body
- No position thoughts
- Find their natural tempo

8. The Count Game

- Count "1-2" for backswing-forward swing
- Vary the count speed
- Feel which option produces best results
- Internalize winning rhythm

9. The Copycat Game

- Copy each other's rhythm (not positions)
- Feel the difference
- Discuss what changed
- Build rhythm awareness

THE FEEL VOCABULARY

Help your child develop language for their feelings:

Distance Feel Words:

- Soft, gentle, smooth
- Firm, solid, strong
- Quick, snappy, explosive
- Easy, flowing, effortless

Contact Feel Words:

- Crispy, pure, clean
- Mushy, thin, fat
- Centered, sweet, solid
- Glancing, sideways, spinny

Rhythm Feel Words:

- Smooth, flowing, rhythmic
- Quick, jabby, rushy
- Patient, waiting, building
- Balanced, centered, stable

Overall Feel Words:

- Free, loose, athletic
- Tight, forced, mechanical
- Natural, easy, flowing
- Controlled, guided, careful

PROTECTING FEEL FROM DESTRUCTION

The Position Police Problem

Every time someone tells your child about a position, they shift from feel to think. Protect them from:

- Technical video analysis
- Position-obsessed instructors
- Well-meaning adults with "tips"
- Social media swing comparisons
- Their own position perfectionism

Creating Feel-Safe Environments

- Choose instructors who speak in feelings and images
- Limit exposure to technical golf content
- Celebrate unique styles
- Focus discussions on ball flight, not body positions
- Make feel the primary language

When Technical Instruction Creeps In

If your child has already been infected with position-thinking:

- Take a complete break from technical work
- Play games focused only on results
- Use feel words exclusively
- Celebrate function over form
- Gradually rebuild feel awareness

FEEL DEVELOPMENT BY SHOT TYPE

Putting Feel

- Rolling versus hitting
- Listening to the ball

- Feeling the green with feet
- Intuitive read trust
- Speed as primary feel

Chipping Feel

- Brushing versus digging
- Landing spot visualization
- Bounce and roll feel
- Touch development
- Natural solutions

Full Swing Feel

- Swoosh location
- Balance awareness
- Rhythm consistency
- Power source feel
- Natural release

THE PARENT'S ROLE IN FEEL DEVELOPMENT

Do:

- Ask about feelings constantly
- Reply using child's feel words
- Celebrate unique solutions
- Focus on results
- Create feel challenges
- Model feel awareness

Don't:

- Don't ever mention positions
- Don't compare to "correct" form
- Don't use technical language
- Don't show technical videos

- Don't praise appearance
- Don't think mechanics

RED FLAGS: WHEN FEEL IS BEING LOST

Watch for these warning signs:

- Swing becomes mechanical
- Multiple swing thoughts
- Paralysis over the ball
- Lost distance/accuracy
- Decreased enjoyment
- Position obsession
- Comparing to others

The Feel Recovery Program

If feel has been compromised:

- Week 1: Complete technical detox—no position talk
- Week 2: Focus on results only for games
- Week 3: Feel vocabulary building
- Week 4: Confidence in natural style returning

CHAPTER 6 ACTION ITEMS

This week, commit to feel development:

- **The Feel Audit**: For one entire practice, count position mentions versus feel discussions. Aim for 0:20 ratio.
- **The Vocabulary Builder**: Help your child create 10 personal feel words for their best shots.
- **The Eyes-Closed Experiment**: Spend 15 minutes hitting various shots with eyes closed. Discuss only feelings.
- **The Feel Journal**: Start documenting your child's feel discoveries in their own words.

SUCCESS STORIES IN FEEL

Maria's Transformation

Nine-year-old Maria had been taught "proper" positions for two years. Her swing looked textbook but produced weak, inconsistent shots. Her parents instituted a feel-only policy. Within two months, Maria discovered her "thunder swing" (her words) that felt powerful and produced amazing results. Her unique style emerged, and her joy returned.

The Thompson Family Method

The Thompsons banned all technical language. Instead, they created feel challenges: "Show me your butterfly shot, your hammer shot, your whisper shot." Their three children developed distinct, effective styles and compete successfully while maintaining pure joy for the game.

THE LONG-TERM FEEL ADVANTAGE

Children who develop feel over mechanics become:

- More creative shot-makers
- Better under pressure
- More adaptable to conditions
- Confident in their style
- Joyful in their play
- Connected to their athleticism
- Lifelong learners

They trust their instincts, solve problems naturally, and maintain the athletic freedom that makes golf a joy rather than a struggle.

YOUR FEEL PHILOSOPHY

Commit to this principle: Your child's feel for the game is sacred. It's their internal guidance system, their athletic wisdom, their connection to joy. Every position instruction damages it. Every feel discovery strengthens it.

Tomorrow, when you practice with your child, bite your tongue when tempted to correct positions. Instead, ask: "How did that feel?" "What did you notice?" "Can you make it feel different?"

Watch them explore. See them discover. Notice their natural athleticism emerge. Celebrate their unique solutions.

Because the child who trusts their feel becomes a golfer who trusts their game. And that trust—not perfect positions—creates greatness.

Remember Mia's rainbow painting discovery from the beginning of this chapter? Years later, she might not remember the technical instructions that confused her, but somewhere inside her, that image remains. Your job is to help her find it again, protect it fiercely, and let it guide her to her own brilliant way of playing this beautiful game.

What feel will your child discover tomorrow?

CHAPTER 7

Games That Build Golf Skills

The Monday afternoon junior clinic looked more like golf boot camp than practice. Twenty children stood in perfect lines, methodically hitting balls with their 7-irons. "Remember, we need one-hundred good swings to build muscle memory," the instructor announced. "Only seventy-three more to go!" The children's expressions ranged from bored to miserable.

Just over the hill, a different scene unfolded. Six young golfers were engaged in what looked like pure chaos—but was actually a brilliant learning design. They were playing "Golf Survivor," where missing a target meant losing a club, forcing creative shot-making with remaining clubs. Laughter mixed with intense concentration as eight-year-old Zoe attempted to hit a high soft shot with only a putter left in her arsenal.

"I figured it out!" she exclaimed, after discovering she could hit the ball on the toe of the putter to create loft. Her playing partners cheered and immediately tried to copy her innovation.

Two groups of children. Both spent an hour at golf practice. Only one group developed real skills—and loved every minute.

This chapter provides you with a comprehensive library of games that build every golf skill while maintaining maximum engagement. You'll learn why games accelerate learning, how to match games to skills and ages, and most importantly, how to create an endless supply of new games that keep practice fresh and exciting.

WHY GAMES ARE LEARNING SUPERPOWERS

Traditional practice treats skill development as work. Games transform it into play. This isn't just about making practice "fun"—games actually produce superior learning through:

Implicit Learning

Games focus attention on outcomes (get ball in target) rather than mechanics (position your arms correctly). This implicit learning creates skills that:

- Survive under pressure
- Transfer to the course
- Adapt to conditions
- Feel natural

Variable Practice

Games inherently create variety—different lies, distances, pressures, and solutions. This variability builds adaptable skills rather than rigid patterns.

Emotional Engagement

Positive emotions during learning enhance:

- Memory formation
- Creative problem-solving
- Motivation to continue
- Deeper understanding

Natural Competition

Games provide appropriate challenge without crushing pressure, building:

- Resilience
- Focus under pressure
- Competitive comfort
- Strategic thinking

THE MASTER GAME LIBRARY

Here are 30 games organized by primary skill development:

Distance Control Games

1. Golf Darts

- Setup: Concentric circles at various distances (hula hoops work great)
- Scoring: Bulls-eye = 5 points, fewer for outer rings
- Skills: Precise distance control, club selection
- Variations: Must call distance first, alternating clubs
- Ages: 6+

2. The Distance Ladder

- Setup: Targets at 10, 20, 30, 40, 50+ yards
- Game: Must hit each distance in order (miss = start over)
- Skills: Progressive distance control, feel development
- Variations: Reverse order, random order, time pressure
- Ages: 8+

3. Goldilocks Golf

- Setup: Three zones: "too short," "just right," "too long"
- Game: Points only for "just right" zone
- Skills: Precision distance, avoiding common misses
- Variations: Shrinking zones, different clubs
- Ages: 7+

4. The Percentage Game

- Setup: One target, multiple power levels
- Game: Hit at 25 percent, 50 percent, 75 percent, 100 percent power
- Skills: Power control, feel development
- Variations: Random percentages, blind calls
- Ages: 10+

Accuracy and Direction Games

5. Golf Bowling

- Setup: 10 targets arranged like bowling pins
- Game: Two shots to knock down all pins
- Skills: Directional precision, strategy
- Variations: Different pin values, obstacles
- Ages: 6+

6. Threading the Needle

- Setup: Two flags/cones creating a "gate"
- Game: Points for shots through the gate
- Skills: Accurate start lines, visualization
- Variations: Narrowing gates, multiple gates
- Ages: 9+

7. Clock Golf

- Setup: Targets arranged like clock numbers
- Game: Instructor calls times, hit to corresponding number
- Skills: Directional awareness, quick adjustment

- Variations: Math problems equal times, speed rounds
- Ages: 8+

8. Battleship Golf

- Setup: Grid system with hidden targets
- Game: Call coordinates, try to hit opponent's ships
- Skills: Precision, strategic thinking
- Variations: Moving ships, different ship sizes
- Ages: 9+

Trajectory Control Games

9. High-Low Challenge

- Setup: Obstacles requiring different trajectories
- Game: Alternate between high and low shots
- Skills: Trajectory control, club selection
- Variations: Random requirements, creativity points
- Ages: 8+

10. Window Washers

- Setup: String/rope creating "windows" at different heights
- Game: Hit shots through specific windows
- Skills: Precise trajectory control
- Variations: Moving windows, multiple windows
- Ages: 10+

11. The Elevator Game

- Setup: Imaginary building with floors
- Game: Hit to specific floors on command
- Skills: Height control, imagination
- Variations: Express vs. local elevator
- Ages: 6+

12. Rainbow Maker

- Setup: Targets requiring arcing shots
- Game: Create the biggest "rainbow" possible
- Skills: Maximum height, soft landing
- Variations: Rainbow contests, color themes
- Ages: 7+

Shot Shaping Games

13. Curve Ball Challenge

- Setup: Obstacles requiring curved shots
- Game: Navigate ball around obstacles
- Skills: Intentional draws/fades
- Variations: Opposite curves, figure-8 patterns
- Ages: 11+

14. The Snake Game

- Setup: Winding path marked on range
- Game: Make ball follow the snake's path
- Skills: Multiple curves, visualization
- Variations: Different snake patterns
- Ages: 12+

15. Shape Master

- Setup: Cards showing different shapes
- Game: Draw card, create that shape
- Skills: Various shot shapes, creativity
- Variations: Partner mimicry, time limits
- Ages: 10+

Short Game Games

16. Chipping Tic-Tac-Toe

- Setup: 9-square grid around green
- Game: Land in square to claim it

- Skills: Precise chipping, strategy
- Variations: Different lies, must call square
- Ages: 7+

17. The Splash Zone

- Setup: Buckets/containers as targets
- Game: Points for direct hits (splashes)
- Skills: Trajectory and distance control
- Variations: Moving targets, different values
- Ages: 6+

18. Around the World Chipping

- Setup: Choose 8 positions around green
- Game: Complete circuit in fewest shots
- Skills: Various lies and distances
- Variations: Worst ball, match play
- Ages: 9+

19. The Bounce Game

- Setup: Specific landing areas marked
- Game: Must bounce exact number of times
- Skills: Spin control, visualization
- Variations: Different surfaces, blind shots
- Ages: 10+

Putting Games

20. Putting Horse

- Setup: Various putting positions
- Game: Copy made putts or get letter
- Skills: Pressure putting, green reading
- Variations: Creative putts allowed
- Ages: 8+

21. Speed Trap

- Setup: Zone past hole for good speed
- Game: Points for stopping in zone
- Skills: Distance control priority
- Variations: Uphill/downhill, teams
- Ages: 7+

22. The Maze

- Setup: Tees creating path to hole
- Game: Navigate through without hitting tees
- Skills: Precision, break reading
- Variations: Time limits, one-shot tries
- Ages: 9+

23. Pressure Ladder

- Setup: Increasing distances to hole
- Game: Make each to advance, miss = restart
- Skills: Pressure management, consistency
- Variations: Lives system, team format
- Ages: 8+

Mental/Strategy Games

24. Course Designer

- Setup: Open range space
- Game: Design holes, play them
- Skills: Strategy, visualization, creativity
- Variations: Theme holes, par requirements
- Ages: 10+

25. Worst Ball Challenge

- Setup: Hit multiple balls
- Game: Must play worst shot
- Skills: Consistency, mental toughness
- Variations: Best ball alternate

- Ages: 11+

26. The Comeback Game

- Setup: Start with terrible lie/position
- Game: Recover in fewest shots
- Skills: Problem-solving, resilience
- Variations: Random bad lies
- Ages: 9+

27. Golf Math

- Setup: Targets with number values
- Game: Hit equation answers
- Skills: Quick thinking, pressure
- Variations: Grade-appropriate math
- Ages: 8+

Team/Social Games

28. Golf Relay Races

- Setup: Teams, multiple challenges
- Game: Race to complete all stations
- Skills: Various, speed, teamwork
- Variations: Different station skills
- Ages: 7+

29. Partner Alternate Shot

- Setup: Teams of two
- Game: Alternate hitting same ball
- Skills: Teamwork, pressure, adaptation
- Variations: Scramble format
- Ages: 9+

30. Golf Tag

- Setup: One person is "it"
- Game: Hit closest to their ball to tag
- Skills: Precision, fun competition
- Variations: Freeze tag rules
- Ages: 6+

CREATING NEW GAMES

The best games often come from children themselves.

Here's the formula:

The Game Creation Formula:

- **Pick a skill** (distance control, accuracy, etc.)
- **Add a challenge** (obstacles, pressure, variety)
- **Create scoring** (points, elimination, racing)
- **Include surprise** (random elements, changes)
- **Name it memorably** (kids love naming games)

Example Creation Process:

- Skill: Trajectory control
- Challenge: Hit over and under alternating
- Scoring: Points for correct trajectory
- Surprise: Spinner determines challenge
- Name: "The Limbo-High Jump Game"

MATCHING GAMES TO DEVELOPMENT

For Beginners (Ages 5-7):

- Maximum imagination elements
- Success broadly defined

- Games last 5-7 minutes
- Rules can change mid-game
- Focus on fun over skill

For Developers (Ages 8-10):

- Clear skill focus
- Moderate challenge
- 10-15 minute games
- Consistent rules
- Competition with self

For Competitors (Ages 11-13):

- Specific skill development
- Pressure elements
- 15-20 minute games
- Strategic elements
- Peer competition

For Performers (Ages 14+):

- Transfer to course
- Mental challenge
- Variable duration
- Self-directed options
- Performance pressure

THE WEEKLY GAME PLAN

Structure variety throughout the week:

Monday: New Game Day

- Introduce 1-2 new games
- Let excitement build
- Focus on learning rules

Wednesday: Challenge Day

- Increase difficulty
- Add pressure elements
- Track improvements

Friday: Fun Day

- Child chooses games
- Mix favorites
- Pure enjoyment focus

Weekend: Application

- Use game skills on course
- Create course games
- Celebrate transfers

CHAPTER 7 ACTION ITEMS

This week, revolutionize practice through games:

- **The Game Test**: Try five new games from this chapter. Note which ones create the most engagement.
- **The Creation Challenge**: Work with your child to invent three original games. Let them lead design.
- **The Skill Audit**: List three skills your child needs to develop. Find or create games for each.
- **The Fun Factor**: Rate each game's fun level (1-10). Only keep games rating 8+.

MAKING GAMES IRRESISTIBLE

The Secret Ingredients:

- **Names**: Kids love games with cool names
- **Props**: Colorful targets, cones, hoops
- **Sound**: Music, effects, celebrations
- **Score**: Visible tracking, achievements
- **Social**: Friends make everything better
- **Choice**: Options within games
- **Surprise**: Unexpected elements

WHEN GAMES WORK MAGIC

You'll know your game approach succeeds when:

- Practice time flies by
- Children create variations
- Skills improve without trying
- Laughter is constant
- You hear them beg for "One more game!"
- Friends want to join
- Golf becomes play

THE GAME-CHANGING TRUTH

Every skill your child needs to develop in golf can be learned through games. Not just learned—but learned better, faster, and with joy that creates lifelong engagement.

The children in that military-style clinic might develop pretty swings through their one hundred repetitions. But Zoe and her friends? They're developing creativity, problem-solving, resilience, and adaptability. They're building skills that transfer to the course and life. Most importantly, they're falling in love with the process of improvement.

Tomorrow, arrive at practice with games, not drills. Watch engagement soar. See skills develop naturally. Hear laughter replace sighs.

Because when children play games, they're not just having fun. They're becoming highly skilled golfers who can adapt, create, and thrive in any situation.

What game will transform your child's practice tomorrow?

CHAPTER 8

Practice Sessions That Work

Six-year-old Ava was crying again. Her Saturday morning practice had started with such promise—she'd bounced out of the car excited to play. But now, after ninety minutes of her well-meaning father's structured session ("Let's hit fifty balls with your 7-iron, then we'll work on your putting stroke"), she was exhausted, frustrated, and declaring she "hated stupid golf."

Meanwhile, on the adjacent hole, eight year old twins Ben and Bailey were having the time of their lives. Their grandmother had created what she called "Golf Adventure Hour"—six different games, each lasting just eight minutes, with stories, challenges, and celebration built in. When their time was up, both children begged for "just five more minutes!"

Same Saturday morning. Same golf course. Completely different experiences.

The difference? One adult understood how to build practice sessions that honor how children actually learn, grow, and thrive. The other was using an adult practice template that ignored everything about child development, attention spans, and joy preservation.

This chapter will transform how you structure practice time with your young golfer. You'll discover the science of session design, learn age-appropriate templates that make practice feel like play, and most importantly, understand how to create sessions your child will beg to continue rather than complain and barely endure.

THE SESSION DESIGN REVOLUTION

Traditional golf practice follows a mind-numbing template: warm up, hit balls, putt, go home. It's designed for adults with developed attention spans, clear goals, and internal motivation. Apply this to children, and you get tears, resistance, and eventually, kids who quit.

Why Traditional Sessions Fail Children:

- The Attention Mismatch
- Adult capacity: 45-90 minutes sustained focus
- Child reality: 5-20 minutes before they require a change
- The Energy Ignorance
- Adult pattern: Steady throughout
- Child pattern: Waves of high and low
- The Motivation Mistake
- Adult driver: Internal goals
- Child driver: Fun and novelty
- The Development Denial
- Adult brain: Fully formed
- Child brain: Rapidly developing, needs variety

UNDERSTANDING ENERGY PATTERNS

Children's energy doesn't flow like adults.' Understanding and working with these patterns transforms practice:

The Energy Wave Pattern:

The Arrival Burst (First 10-15 percent)

- Highest excitement
- Maximum openness
- Prime learning window
- Capture immediately

The Focus Peak (Next 40-50 percent)

- Deepest engagement
- Best skill work
- Challenge acceptance
- Progress visible

The Fade Phase (Next 25-30 percent)

- Attention wandering
- Fatigue showing
- Mistakes increasing
- Shift needed

The Final Push (Last 10-15 percent)

- Second wind possible
- If activity changes
- Ending strong is essential
- Memory cement time

AGE-SPECIFIC SESSION TEMPLATES

Great practice sessions match the child's developmental stage perfectly:

Ages 5-7: The Magic Window (20-30 minutes max)

The 20-Minute Wonder Session

Minutes 0-3: Excitement Upon Arrival

- Free play with clubs
- No instruction
- Build energy
- "What should we try today?"

Minutes 3-8: Game One– The Adventure Begins

- Story-based challenge
- "Pirates searching for treasure"
- Multiple clubs used
- Success guaranteed

Minutes 8-11: The Energy Shift

- Completely different activity
- Maybe switch from putting to chipping
- New story/theme
- Keep momentum

Minutes 11-16: Game Two – The Challenge Grows

- Slightly harder task
- Still wrapped in play
- Celebrate attempts
- No position focus

Minutes 16-18: The Victory Lap

- Child's choice activity
- Usually their favorite
- End on high note
- Leave them wanting more

Minutes 18-20: The Celebration Circle

- Review discoveries
- High fives abundant
- Plan next adventure
- Pack up together

Key Principles:

- Never extend past energy
- Story drives everything
- Success is broadly defined
- Positions never mentioned
- Joy is the only metric

Ages 8-10: The Skill Explosion Era (30-45 minutes)

The 45-Minute Explorer Session

Minutes 0-5: The Dynamic Start

- Active warmup game
- "Distance ladder" or "target race"
- Get blood flowing
- Build excitement

Minutes 5-15: Skill Station One

- Focus on one area
- Game-based learning
- "Shape master challenge"
- Track progress playfully

Minutes 15-20: The Brain Break

- Water and snack
- Share discoveries
- Quick energy game
- Reset attention

Minutes 20-30: Skill Station Two

- Different skill entirely
- New games/challenges
- Maintain novelty
- Build on energy

Minutes 30-38: The Integration Game

- Combine skills learned
- "Golf obstacle course"
- Creativity encouraged
- Fun competition

Minutes 38-42: The Pressure Finale

- One pressure challenge
- Age-appropriate stakes
- Celebrate courage
- Quick and positive

Minutes 42-45: The Reflection Ritual

- What worked well?
- Favorite moment?
- Tomorrow's dream?
- Pack with purpose

Key Principles:

- Stations prevent boredom
- Breaks recharge batteries
- Integration solidifies learning
- Pressure builds resilience
- Reflection cements memories

Ages 11-13: The Competitive Awakening (45-60 minutes)

The 60-Minute Competitor Session

Minutes 0-8: The Performance Prep

- Dynamic warmup
- Include competition movements
- Mental preparation
- "Today's mission..."

Minutes 8-20: Technical Block

- One skill deep dive
- Film for self-analysis
- External focus cues
- Quality over quantity

Minutes 20-35: Variable Practice Block

- Random club selection
- Course simulation
- Decision training
- "What would you do?"

Minutes 35-40: The Reset

- Complete break
- Hydration/nutrition
- Social connection
- Energy management

Minutes 40-52: Competition Block

- Matches with consequences
- Pressure situations
- Score tracking
- Mental game work

Minutes 52-60: The Champion's Review

- Statistical analysis (fun)
- Video highlights
- Goal adjustment
- Next session planning

Key Principles:

- Blocks allow deeper work
- Competition normalized
- Self-analysis develops
- Pressure integrated naturally
- Ownership increasing

Ages 14+: The Ownership Years (60-90 minutes)

The 90-Minute Mastery Session

Minutes 0-10: The Professional Prep

- Student leads warm-up
- Parent observes/supports
- Mental game activation
- Session goals stated

Minutes 10-30: Priority Block

- Biggest improvement area
- Mixture of activities
- Self-directed discovery
- Parent as resource

Minutes 30-45: Transfer Training

- Course-like conditions
- Pressure integration
- Decision emphasis
- Reality simulation

Minutes 45-50: The Strategic Break

- Nutrition/hydration
- Mental reset
- Energy assessment
- Plan adjustment

Minutes 50-70: Performance Block

- Competition preparation
- Specific scenarios
- Mental routines
- Clutch practice

Minutes 70-85: Creative Block

- Experimentation time
- New shots/techniques
- Risk-taking is safe
- Innovation celebrated

Minutes 85-90: The Professional Debrief

- Data review
- Video analysis
- Planning together
- Mutual respect

READING ENERGY SIGNALS

Successful sessions require reading your child's energy state:

Green Light Signals:

- Animated movement
- Asking questions
- Trying variations
- Smiling/laughing
- "Watch this!"

Yellow Light Signals:

- Slowing pace
- Less enthusiasm
- Routine responses
- Checking time
- "How much longer?"

Red Light Signals:

- Frustration growing
- Negative body language
- Mistakes multiplying
- Engagement gone
- "I want to go home"

Response Strategies:

- Green: Push appropriately
- Yellow: Change activity
- Red: End immediately

CREATING YOUR WEEKLY RHYTHM

Build sustainable practice patterns:

The Three-Session Week (Minimum Effective Dose)

- Monday: Skill focus (30-45 min)
- Wednesday: Game day (30-45 min)
- Saturday: Course play or extended session

The Five-Session Week (Engaged Player)

- Monday: Technical work
- Tuesday: Short game
- Thursday: Competition prep
- Friday: Fun/creative
- Weekend: Course play

The Daily Touch (Passionate Player)

- 15-20 minutes daily
- Different focus each day
- One mandatory rest day
- Course play counts
- Quality over quantity

ENVIRONMENTAL FACTORS

Where and when you practice matters:

Location Variety:

- Home practice area
- Driving range
- Short game facility
- On-course practice
- Creative spaces

Timing Considerations:

- Energy peaks (varies by child)
- Weather comfort
- Social availability
- School schedule
- Family balance

Atmosphere Creation:

- Music for energy
- Props for fun
- Friends for motivation
- Challenges for engagement
- Celebration built in

THE SESSION PLANNING SYSTEM

Pre-Session (5 minutes before)

- Check child's energy
- Confirm session length
- Review planned activities
- Adjust if needed
- Set joyful tone

During Session:

- Watch energy closely
- Adjust on the fly
- Celebrate constantly
- Allow child input
- Maintain flexibility

Post-Session (5 minutes after)

- Quick wins review
- Child's favorite part
- Parent observation
- Next session teaser
- Positive ending

COMMON SESSION MISTAKES

Mistake 1: The Marathon Mentality

- Sessions are too long
- Energy depleted
- Negative associations
- Solution: Multiple short beats one long

Mistake 2: The Adult Template

- Boring structure
- Lost engagement

- Practice resistance
- Solution: Age-appropriate design

Mistake 3: The Rigid Schedule

- Ignoring energy levels
- Forcing bad sessions
- Creating obligation
- Solution: Flexibility rules

Mistake 4: The Position Prison

- Technical overload
- Mechanical players
- Lost athleticism
- Solution: Games and external focus

CHAPTER 8 ACTION ITEMS

This week, transform your practice sessions:

- **The Energy Tracking**: For three sessions, note your child's energy patterns. Find their optimal duration.
- **The Template Test**: Use the age-appropriate template from this chapter. Note what works best.
- **The Flexibility Experiment**: Plan a session but adjust it based on your child's energy. Notice the difference.
- **The Joy Measurement**: Rate fun level (1-10) for each part of practice. Adjust until consistently 8+.

SUCCESS STORIES

The Garcia Family Transformation

The Garcias struggled with three children (ages six, nine, and twelve) who were all resisting practice. Dad's one-size-fits-all sessions weren't working. After implementing age-specific templates:

- 6-year-old: 20-minute adventures
- 9-year-old: 45-minute game rotations
- 12-year-old: 60-minute competition prep

Result: All three now ask for more practice time.

Emma's Energy Revolution Eight-year-old Emma was labeled "unfocused" during morning lessons. Her parents discovered she peaked from 4-6 p.m. They shifted practice to after school, shortened sessions to thirty-five minutes, and packed them with variety. Emma transformed into an engaged, enthusiastic player.

THE LONG VIEW

Remember: Every practice session is writing a page in your child's golf story. Make those pages filled with:

- Discovery and laughter
- Growth and joy
- Challenge and support
- Energy and engagement
- Reminders to:Avoid tedium and frustration
- Just say no to pressure and tears
- Not boredom and resistance
- Prevent exhaustion and resentment

YOUR SESSION REVOLUTION STARTS NOW

Tomorrow, instead of arriving at practice with vague plans and adult expectations, arrive with:

- Age-appropriate structure
- Energy awareness
- Flexible mindset
- Games ready to adapt
- Joy as priority

Watch your child transform from reluctant participant to eager player. See practice become anticipated rather than endured. Notice skills developing naturally through engagement.

Because when practice sessions honor how children actually learn and grow, magic happens. Golf becomes not something they have to do, but something they can't wait to do.

What kind of session will you create tomorrow?

PART III

THE MENTAL AND EMOTIONAL GAME

CHAPTER 9

Building Confidence and Resilience

The junior club championship was down to the final hole. Thirteen-year-old Emma stood over a four-foot putt to win her first tournament. Her hands trembled. Her mind raced with doubt: "What if I miss? Everyone's watching. I can't do this." The putt that she'd made hundreds of times in practice slipped by the edge. She ran to her mother in tears, convinced she was "terrible at golf" and "would never win anything."

Two weeks later, at the next event, eleven-year-old Carlos faced the same situation—four feet to win. But Carlos had been raised differently. When doubts crept in, he heard his grandfather's voice: "You've made this putt before. Trust your stroke. Whatever happens, I'm proud of you." Carlos took a deep breath, smiled, and rolled the putt dead center.

Two children. Two pressure moments. Two completely different inner dialogues.

The difference wasn't talent or technique. It was confidence—that deep, unshakeable belief in one's ability to handle whatever golf throws your way. This chapter will show you how to build that confidence in your child, along with its essential partner: resilience, the ability to bounce back from golf's inevitable setbacks.

UNDERSTANDING CONFIDENCE IN YOUNG GOLFERS

Confidence isn't about never doubting—it's about trusting your ability despite doubts. For young golfers, confidence develops through:

The Confidence Building Blocks:

- **Competence**: Actual skill development
- **Experience**: Successful past references
- **Support**: Unconditional backing
- **Perspective**: Healthy view of "failure"
- **Autonomy**: Ownership of their game

When any block is missing, confidence crumbles under pressure.

THE CONFIDENCE KILLERS

Before building confidence, we must stop destroying it:

Comparison to Others

Every time you mention how well another child plays, you plant seeds of inadequacy. Your child hears: "You're not good enough as you are."

Perfectionism Pressure

Expecting mistake-free golf creates paralysis. Children become afraid to try, knowing they'll inevitably fall short.

Outcome Obsession

When scores matter more than effort, children learn their worth depends on results they can't fully control.

Technical Overload

Constant position corrections create self-doubt. Children lose trust in their natural abilities.

Conditional Approval

When your mood depends on their performance, children play to avoid disappointment rather than seek joy.

THE ULTIMATE CONFIDENCE KILLER: CONDITIONAL LOVE

Nothing destroys a child's confidence faster than sensing their worth in your eyes depends on their performance. This creates a devastating cycle:

The Cycle of Conditional Love:

- Child senses love is tied to performance
- Pressure intensifies exponentially
- Fear of failure paralyzes natural ability
- Performance suffers under pressure
- Child feels less loved
- Confidence crumbles further
- Cycle repeats and deepens

Breaking the Cycle:

- Explicitly state love is unconditional
- Prove it through consistent behavior
- Celebrate courage over outcomes
- Share your own failures openly
- Give physical affection after every round
- Display same energy regardless of scores

Remember: A child who knows they're loved unconditionally has unshakeable confidence because their worth isn't on the line with every shot.

BUILDING TRUE CONFIDENCE

Real confidence comes from within and builds gradually:

Ages 5-8: Foundation Years

At this age, confidence is about feeling capable and loved:

Daily Builders:

- "I love watching you play"
- "You figured that out!"
- "Look how far you hit that!"
- "You're getting stronger!"

Experience Creation:

- Set up easy successes
- Celebrate small wins
- Create "personal bests"
- Document progress visually

Mistake Handling:

- "Good try! What did you learn?"
- "Everyone misses sometimes"
- "Let's try again!"
- Model mistake recovery

Story of Success: Seven-year-old Lily was terrified of hitting over water. Her dad created "stepping stones"—starting with a tiny puddle, then a small pond, gradually building to real water hazards. Each success built upon the last. Six months later, Lily eagerly attacked water holes, remembering all her victories.

Ages 9-12: Growth Years

Confidence becomes more complex as social awareness grows:

Competence Building:

- Master fundamental skills
- Create specialty shots
- Develop "go-to" techniques
- Build course management

Internal Dialog Development:

- Teach positive self-talk
- Create personal mantras
- Develop pre-shot routines
- Build focusing techniques

Pressure Inoculation:

- Start with tiny pressures
- Gradually increase stakes
- Celebrate courage, not just success
- Normalize nervousness

The Confidence Bank Account

Help your child create a "confidence bank"—a journal of successes:

- Great shots hit
- Problems solved
- Courage shown
- Progress made
- Fun moments

Before big events, make "withdrawals" by reviewing entries.

Ages 13-16: Testing Years

Confidence faces its biggest challenges as competition intensifies:

Identity Separation:

Help them understand: "You are not your golf score"

- Value multiple attributes
- Celebrate character
- Recognize other talents
- Maintain perspective

Process Confidence:

Shift focus from outcome confidence ("I can win") to process confidence ("I can execute my routine"):

- Trust preparation
- Control controllables
- Accept outcomes
- Learn constantly

Peer Pressure Navigation:

- Choose supportive peer groups
- Avoid toxic comparisons
- Celebrate unique journey
- Model confidence

BUILDING RESILIENCE:

THE BOUNCE-BACK FACTOR

Resilience—recovering from setbacks—matters more than avoiding them:

The Resilience Formula

Setback + Support + Perspective + Action = Growth

When children experience this formula repeatedly, they develop unshakeable resilience.

Teaching Healthy Failure Response

The 24-Hour Rule:

After a disappointing round:

- First hour: Feel the feelings
- Next hours: Distraction and care
- Next day: Gentle reflection
- Within a week: Back to joy

The Learning Frame:

Transform setbacks into education:

- "What did this teach us?"
- "How will this help next time?"
- "What would you do differently?"
- "What actually went well?"

The Bounce-Back Plan:

Create a family protocol for disappointments:

- Acknowledge feelings
- Provide comfort
- Maintain perspective
- Find the lessons
- Create action plan
- Return to fun

PRACTICAL CONFIDENCE BUILDERS

The Success Highlight Reel

Create a video compilation of your child's best moments:

- Great shots
- Courage displays
- Fun celebrations
- Progress markers

Watch before challenging events.

The Strength Spotter

Weekly, identify three strengths your child displayed:

- "Your attitude after that bad hole was amazing"
- "You helped your playing partner—that's leadership"
- "You tried that difficult shot—that's courage"

The Growth Chart

Track improvement beyond scores:

- Shots attempted (courage)
- Recovery shots (resilience)
- Good decisions (wisdom)
- Calling penalty (character)

The Pressure Practice Progression

Week 1: Personal challenges only Week 2: Parent watching Week 3: Friend competing Week 4: Small audience Week 5: Stakes added Week 6: Tournament simulation

Build pressure immunity gradually.

AGE-APPROPRIATE RESILIENCE ACTIVITIES

Ages 5-8: Story-Based Resilience

- Read books about overcoming challenges
- Create golf adventure stories where heroes face setbacks
- Act out recovering from bad shots
- Celebrate "brave tries"

Ages 9-12: Skill-Based Resilience

- "Worst ball" challenges (play worst shot, recover)
- "Disaster recovery" games
- Share your own failure stories
- Team resilience activities

Ages 13+: Mental Training

- Visualization of recovery
- Breathing techniques
- Refocusing routines
- Resilience mentors

THE PARENT'S ROLE IN CONFIDENCE BUILDING

Your Words Matter:

Instead of: "Don't be nervous" Say: "It's normal to feel butterflies. They help you focus!"

Instead of: "You should have made that" Say: "You'll make the next one"

Instead of: "Why did you do that?" Say: "What were you thinking there?" (with curiosity, not judgment)

Your Energy Matters More:

Children read your non-verbal cues:

- Relaxed posture says "I'm not worried"
- Smile says "This is fun"
- Calm voice says "All is well"
- Consistent mood says "You're loved regardless"

WHEN CONFIDENCE CRACKS

Warning signs of eroding confidence:

- Avoiding challenges
- Excessive self-criticism
- Physical symptoms (stomachaches)
- Lost enthusiasm
- Comparison obsession

The Confidence Restoration Plan:

- Reduce all pressure immediately
- Return to pure fun
- Create easy successes
- Rebuild slowly
- Address root causes
- Seek help if needed

BUILDING LONG-TERM MENTAL TOUGHNESS

True mental toughness isn't about being hard—it's about being adaptable:

The Four Pillars:

- **Emotional Awareness**: Recognizing and accepting feelings
- **Coping Skills**: Tools for managing difficulty
- **Growth Mindset**: Seeing challenges as opportunities
- **Support Seeking**: Knowing when to ask for help

CHAPTER 9 ACTION ITEMS

This week, build confidence and resilience:

1. **The Strength Safari**: Each day, "catch" your child doing something well. Share it at dinner.
2. **The Mistake Celebration**: When your child makes a mistake, help them find the lesson. Celebrate the learning.
3. **The Confidence Journal**: Start documenting successes, both large and small. Review weekly.
4. **The Pressure Practice**: Add one small pressure element to practice. Notice how your child responds.

SUCCESS STORIES IN RESILIENCE

Jake's Journey Due to nerves, 10-year-old Jake cried before every tournament. His parents implemented a gradual pressure-building program:

- Week 1: Putting contests with sister
- Week 2: Chipping games with stakes
- Week 3: Nine holes counting score
- Month 2: Local junior events
- Month 3: Comfortable competing

Jake now says: "I still get nervous, but I know I can handle it."

The Martinez Method

The Martinez family created "Failure Friday"—one day a week where everyone shared a mistake and what they learned. Golf failures became normalized as part of learning. Their daughter went from quitting after bad shots to saying, "Well, that's my Failure Friday story!"

THE ULTIMATE TRUTH ABOUT CONFIDENCE

Confidence doesn't come from never failing—it comes from knowing you can handle failure. It doesn't come from being the best—it comes from being your best. It doesn't come from perfection—it comes from self-acceptance.

Your role isn't to protect your child from every setback. It's to be their safe harbor when setbacks come. It's to help them see failure as information, not identity. It's to build their confidence and belief system. The lesson learned is that there will be struggles, but they can handle any struggle.

YOUR DAILY CONFIDENCE MISSION

Tomorrow, commit to:

- Finding three things to praise (effort, attitude, courage)
- Responding to mistakes with curiosity, not criticism
- Sharing a story of your own resilience
- Celebrating progress, however small
- Ending the day with "I love watching you play"

Because confident children don't become that way by accident. They're built through thousands of small moments where they felt capable, supported, and valued for who they are, not what they score.

Remember Emma from our opening story? Her parents read this chapter and transformed their approach. Six months later, she faced another pressure putt. This time, her inner dialogue was different: "I've prepared for this. I can handle whatever happens. This is fun!"

She made it—but more importantly, she knew she would have been okay if she hadn't.

That's the confidence and resilience you're helping them build. Not the kind that depends on makes or misses, but the kind that weathers any storm and emerges stronger.

What confidence will you build in your child tomorrow?

CHAPTER 10

Handling Pressure and Competition

The scoreboard at the regional junior championship told only part of the story. What it didn't show was twelve-year-old Michael in the parking lot, refusing to get out of the car. "I can't do it," he sobbed. "Everyone will be watching. What if I mess up?" His parents exchanged worried glances. Their talented son, who played beautifully at home, became paralyzed when it "counted."

Meanwhile, ten-year-old Zara was on the first tee, bouncing with excitement. "This is just like our Sunday pressure games!" she told her dad. "Except with more people watching—that makes it even more fun!" She'd faced pressure so often in practice that competition felt familiar, even comfortable.

Two children. Equal talent. Completely different relationships with competitive pressure.

This chapter reveals how to help your child not just survive competitive pressure, but thrive in it. You'll learn why some children crumble while others excel when stakes rise, and most importantly, how to build pressure immunity through progressive, playful exposure.

UNDERSTANDING PRESSURE IN YOUNG ATHLETES

Pressure isn't inherently bad—it's neutral energy that can enhance or destroy performance depending on how children interpret it. The physical sensations are identical to excitement: increased heart rate, heightened awareness, adrenaline flow. The difference lies in the story they tell themselves.

The Pressure Paradox

Children who never experience pressure in practice will inevitably crumble in competition. But children thrown into high-pressure situations too early may develop competition anxiety that lasts a lifetime. The key is progressive, appropriate exposure—like building immunity through small, controlled doses.

WHY TRADITIONAL APPROACHES FAIL

The "Just Relax" Myth

Telling an anxious child to "just relax" is like saying to someone afraid of heights, "just don't look down." It doesn't work and often increases anxiety by making them feel they're failing at relaxing too.

The Sink-or-Swim Mistake

Throwing children into highly competitive events hoping they'll "figure it out" often creates trauma, not toughness. Without preparation, they associate competition with fear and failure.

The Avoidance Trap

Protecting children from all pressure seems kind but leaves them utterly unprepared for life's inevitable competitive moments—in golf and beyond.

THE PROGRESSIVE PRESSURE SYSTEM

Like teaching swimming, pressure immunity develops through careful progression:

Level 1: Pressure in Private (Ages 5-8)

Start with tiny stakes in safe environments:

Personal Challenges:

- "Can you make three putts in a row?"
- "Try to hit five balls past the marker"
- "Chip three in the circle"

Key Elements:

- Self-imposed pressure only
- Multiple attempts allowed
- Parent as cheerleader
- Celebration of attempts

Games That Build Early Pressure Immunity:

The Countdown Game

- Give them 10 balls to hit a target
- Countdown creates mild pressure
- Success = any hits
- Focus on fun under time constraint

The Prize Putt

- Make this putt = choose dessert
- Miss = parent chooses (still fun option)
- Stakes matter but aren't crushing
- Builds pressure association with fun

Level 2: Social Pressure (Ages 8-10)

Add the element of others watching:

Peer Pressure Introduction:

- Practice games with friends
- Parents watching occasionally
- Small audiences (siblings, grandparents)
- Performance for others normalized

Competition Concepts:

- Keeping score together
- Winning and losing in games
- Supporting competitors
- Handling both outcomes

Pressure-Building Games:

The Challenge Match

- Best of 5 competitions
- Various skills tested
- Audience encourages both players
- Post-match high-fives mandatory

Team Pressure

- Friendly competition with teammate with similar skill level
- Shared success/failure

- Mutual support developed
- Pressure distributed

Level 3: Competition Introduction (Ages 11-13)

Introduce formal competitive elements:

Mock and Local Tournaments:

- Create "official" events at home
- Enroll child in local tour events
- Small trophies or ribbons
- Ceremony and recognition

Pressure Practice Protocols:

- Must announce shot intention
- One ball only (no mulligans)
- Consequences for outcomes
- Time constraints added

Mental Preparation Introduction:

- Pre-shot routines developed
- Breathing techniques taught
- Visualization introduced
- Self-talk strategies

Advanced Pressure Games:

The Elimination Round

- Multiple players start
- Bottom score eliminated for each hole
- Pressure increases naturally
- Survival mentality built

The Money Game (with pennies or points)

- Each shot has value
- Running tallies kept
- Pressure of protecting lead
- Experience gaining ground

Level 4: Real Competition (Ages 14+)

Transfer practice pressure to actual events:

Tournament Preparation:

- Simulate tournament conditions
- Practice with strangers watching
- Handle delays and distractions
- Manage emotions actively

Tournament Participation:

- Enroll child in regional events
- Begin keeping tournament portfolio results
- Test national level tournaments depending on skill
- Begin keeping a golf college journal for coaches

Advanced Mental Skills:

- Complex pre-shot routines
- Pressure breathing patterns
- Competition visualization
- Post-round processing

READING YOUR CHILD'S PRESSURE RESPONSE

Every child responds differently to pressure. Understanding your child's pattern helps you support appropriately:

The Fighter

- Rises to challenges
- Performs better under pressure
- Seeks competitive situations
- Needs: Appropriate challenges, not protection

The Freezer

- Paralyzed by pressure
- Mind goes blank
- Physical tension is extreme
- Needs: Gradual exposure, coping tools

The Fleer

- Avoids pressure situations
- Makes excuses
- Develops mystery illnesses
- Needs: Safe pressure experiences, choice

The Fluctuator

- Inconsistent pressure response
- Good days and bad days
- Emotional volatility
- Needs: Stability, routine, patience

COMPETITION PREPARATION STRATEGIES

The Week Before

Normalize, Don't Minimize:

- "It's normal to feel excited/nervous"
- "Your butterflies help you focus"
- "Everyone feels this way"
- Avoid: "It's no big deal"

Preparation Focus:

- Practice tournament routine
- Play practice rounds
- Maintain normal schedule
- Avoid major changes

Confidence Building:

- Review past successes
- Practice favorite shots
- Positive visualization
- Strength reminders
- Tournament Day

Morning Routine:

- Familiar breakfast
- Normal timing
- Calming music
- Positive energy

Warm-up Protocol:

- Start with best clubs
- Build confidence gradually
- Avoid problem areas
- End on good note

Parent Energy:

- Calm and confident
- Excited, not anxious
- Present, not hovering
- Supportive, not coaching

DURING COMPETITION SUPPORT

What to Say:

- "I love watching you compete"
- "Trust your practice"
- "One shot at a time"
- "You're prepared for this"
- "Have fun out there"

What NOT to Say:

- "Don't be nervous"
- "You need to score well"
- "Everyone's watching"
- "This is important"
- "Don't mess up"

Between Holes:

- Quick positive touch
- Water and fuel reminder
- Simple encouragement
- No technical advice
- Reset and refocus

POST-COMPETITION PROCESSING

The hour after competition shapes future attitudes:

Immediate Response (First 30 minutes):

- Congratulate on courage to compete
- Food and hydration first
- No score analysis

- Emotional support only
- "I'm proud of you"

Later Processing (That evening):

- "What was fun today?"
- "What did you learn?"
- "What made you proud?"
- "What would you do again?"
- Focus on positives first

Next Day Reflection:

- Review without judgment
- Find growth areas together
- Celebrate improvements
- Plan next steps
- Maintain perspective

CRITICAL WARNING: POST-COMPETITION LOVE

The hour after competition is when children are most vulnerable to feeling conditional love. Your reaction in this window can either reinforce their worth or tie it to their score forever.

SAME love after shooting 65 or 95 SAME hug after winning or losing

SAME smile after birdies or bogeys SAME dinner conversation after any result

If you can't manage this, stay home. Your conditional reactions would cause more damage than missing their round would cause disappointment.

BUILDING COMPETITIVE RESILIENCE

The Bounce-Back Protocol

When competition goes poorly:

1. **Acknowledge Feelings**: "I see you're disappointed. That's okay."
2. **Provide Perspective**: "Everyone has tough days."
3. **Find One Positive**: "Your attitude on 15 was amazing."
4. **Focus Forward**: "What's one thing to work on?"
5. **Return to Fun**: "Let's play a fun round tomorrow."

Creating Competitive Memories

Build positive associations with competition:

- Tournament trip traditions
- Special meals after events
- Photo albums of fun moments
- Stories of courage, not just scores
- Friendships made at events

AGE-APPROPRIATE COMPETITION GUIDELINES

Ages 5-7:

- Fun, team formats only
- No individual stroke play
- Modified rules allowed
- Everyone gets recognition
- Parent caddies welcome

Ages 8-10:

- Begin individual events
- Local competitions only
- Limit to 1-2 per month
- Maximum of 9 holes
- Focus on experience

Ages 11-13:

- Regional competitions possible
- Gradually introduce 18 holes
- Monthly events reasonable
- Rankings de-emphasized
- Process goals primary

Ages 14+:

- Full competitive schedule possible
- National events if desired
- College prep considered
- Individual goals drive schedule
- Burnout prevention is crucial

CHAPTER 10 ACTION ITEMS

This week, build pressure immunity:

1. **The Pressure Assessment**: Identify your child's pressure response type. Design support accordingly.
2. **The Home Tournament**: Create a fun, official competition at home. Include ceremonies and prizes.
3. **The Pressure Game Introduction**: Add one new pressure game to practice. Start small.
4. **The Competition Conversation**: Discuss what makes competition fun vs. scary. Listen without fixing.

RED FLAGS IN COMPETITION

Watch for signs competition has become harmful:

Physical Symptoms:

- Persistent stomach issues
- Sleep disruption before events
- Appetite loss
- Headaches increasing

Emotional Symptoms:

- Dread before events
- Tears becoming common
- Anger outbursts
- Withdrawal from golf

Behavioral Changes:

- Avoiding practice
- Making excuses
- Cheating temptations
- Lost joy completely

If you see these signs, immediately:

- Reduce competition schedule
- Return to fun golf only
- Seek professional help if needed
- Prioritize mental health

SUCCESS STORIES

The Thompson Family Method

The Thompsons created "Family Olympics" every Sunday—silly competitions with made-up events. Their kids learned to love pressure in a safe environment. When real tournaments came, their daughter said, "This is easier than Dad's crazy challenges!"

Carlos's Transformation

Remember Carlos from earlier? His grandfather's secret was simple: every practice included one "pressure putt" for something fun— picking the music in the car, choosing the movie, earning extra range balls. By tournament time, pressure equaled opportunity, not threat.

THE ULTIMATE COMPETITION TRUTH

Competition is a tool, not a destination. Used wisely, it builds character, resilience, and joy. Used poorly, it destroys childhood, relationships, and love for the game.

The best competitors aren't always those who play the most tournaments. They're often those who compete with joy, maintain balance, own their journey, and see tournaments as fun challenges rather than identity tests.

Your child can experience the benefits of competition without sacrificing their childhood. The key is remembering that they're children first, golfers second, and your beloved child always—regardless of any scorecard.

Tomorrow, if your child asks about competing, you'll be ready. Not with rigid rules, but with wisdom about what serves them best. You'll know how to create competitive experiences that build rather than break, enhance rather than consume, and always—always—protect the joy that brought them to golf in the first place.

What kind of competitive journey will you choose together?

CHAPTER 11

When Challenges Arise

The text came at 10 p.m. on a Tuesday: "We need to talk. Maya wants to quit golf."

Just six months earlier, nine year old Maya had been the picture of golf joy—bouncing to the first tee, creating imaginative games on the range, begging for extra practice time. Now she was in tears before every session, complaining of stomachaches on tournament days, and had just declared she "never wanted to see another golf club again."

Her parents were devastated. They'd invested time, money, and dreams into Maya's golf journey. Where had they gone wrong? What could they do? Was this the end?

Meanwhile, across town, the Thompson family was navigating their own crisis. Their eleven-year-old son, Jake, had been stuck at the same skill level for eight months. Despite increased practice, new instructors, and expensive equipment, nothing seemed to help. His frustration was building, and his parents were running out of ideas—and patience.

Two families. Two different challenges. Two stories that are repeated in junior golf families around the world.

This chapter is your guide for navigating the inevitable challenges in your child's golf journey. You'll learn to recognize warning signs before they become crises, implement specific solutions for common problems, and most importantly, maintain perspective when the path gets rocky.

UNDERSTANDING THE CHALLENGE LANDSCAPE

Every young golfer's journey includes challenges. The difference between those who persist and those who quit isn't the absence of difficulties—it's how families navigate them.

The Challenge Timeline:

- **Year 1**: Honeymoon phase, few serious challenges
- **Years 2-3**: First plateaus and frustrations emerge
- **Years 4-5**: Comparison pressure intensifies
- **Years 6+**: Burnout risk peaks

Being aware of this timeline and typical peaks and valleys helps you prepare for and normalize challenges when they arise.

THE FIVE MAJOR CHALLENGE CATEGORIES

1. The "I Want to Quit" Crisis

This is the most heart-wrenching challenge parents face. But not all "I quit" declarations are equal:

Level 1: The Momentary Meltdown

- Triggered by bad round/practice
- Highly emotional but brief
- Usually includes tears or anger
- Resolves within hours/days
- Child returns willingly

Parent Response:

- Acknowledge feelings: "I see you're really frustrated"
- Give space: "Let's take a break"
- Don't overreact or negotiate
- Revisit when calm
- Focus on immediate comfort

Level 2: The Burnout Warning

- Building over months
- Decreased enthusiasm
- Excuses to skip practice
- Joy noticeably absent
- Performance declining

Parent Response:

- Immediate schedule reduction
- Return to pure fun in golf practices
- Remove all pressure
- Explore root causes
- Major adjustments required

Level 3: The Complete Rejection

- Sustained over many months
- Physical symptoms (headaches, stomach issues)
- Anxiety/depression signs
- Complete activity avoidance
- Impacts other life areas

Parent Response:

- Full stop on golf
- Consider professional help
- Address mental health first
- No guilt or pressure
- Complete reset needed

The Comeback Protocol:

Week 1-2: Complete Break

- No golf at all
- No golf talk
- Fun alternative activities
- Reconnect as a family

Week 3-4: Gentle Reintroduction

- "Want to hit some balls?"
- No pressure to continue
- Make it their choice
- Focus on fun only

Week 5-6: Rebuild Foundation

- Games only if continuing
- New environment/partners
- Celebrate tiny wins
- Let them lead

Week 7-8: Future Visioning

- "What would make golf fun?"
- Create new approach together
- Set boundaries
- Make commitment flexible

2. The Dreaded Plateau

When progress stalls, frustration builds:

Understanding Plateaus:

- Normal part of development
- Often precede breakthroughs
- Brain is consolidating learning
- Body adapting to changes

Types of Plateaus:

The Consolidation Plateau (4-8 weeks)

- Brain organizing new patterns
- Maintain course, trust process
- Breakthrough often sudden

The Transition Plateau (2-6 months)

- Growth spurts, technique changes
- Adjust expectations
- Support through changes

The Burnout Plateau (Indefinite)

- Overtraining, pressure, joy loss
- Major intervention required
- Address root causes first

Plateau-Busting Strategies:

1. **Change the Metric**
   - Stop measuring score
   - Track creativity, recovery, joy
   - Celebrate different achievements

2. **Radical Variety**
   - Switch to completely different courses
   - Introduce new practice games
   - Change to new playing partners
   - Experiment with alternative golf formats
3. **The Opposite Week**
   - Opposite hand putting
   - Backward course playing
   - Night golf adventures
   - Anything different
4. **Goal Revolution**
   - Abandon outcome goals
   - Create process adventures
   - Focus on experiences
   - Remove all comparisons

3. Social and Peer Challenges

Golf's individual nature doesn't protect from social dynamics:

Common Scenarios:

The Comparison Trap

- "Everyone's better than me"
- Constant ranking checks
- Self-worth determined through golf
- Friendship competition

Solution:

- Ban ranking discussions
- Focus on personal journey
- Find supportive peer groups
- Celebrate uniqueness

The Equipment Arms Race

- "I need what they have"
- Status through stuff
- Constant upgrades
- Parent pressure

Solution:

- Set clear boundaries
- Focus on skill over gear
- Earn through effort
- Value creativity

The Practice Shame

- "I don't practice enough"
- Guilt and inadequacy
- Quantity obsession
- Joy depletion

Solution:

- Quality over quantity
- Share your values
- Find like-minded families
- Build confidence in approach

4. Physical and Technical Challenges

Growth Spurts:

- Coordination disruption
- Power changes
- Flexibility issues
- Frustration peaks

Management:

- Expect temporary regression
- Adjust expectations
- Focus on athleticism
- Patience is essential

Injury Concerns:

- Overuse risks
- Growth plate issues
- Flexibility imbalances
- Burnout correlation

Prevention:

- Encourage adding another sport
- Rest days mandatory
- Flexibility programs
- Listen to pain

Technical Confusion:

- Multiple instructors
- Conflicting advice
- Lost natural swing
- Paralysis by analysis

Solution:

- One trusted instructor
- Feel over positions
- Video comparison limited
- Return to athletics

5. Family Dynamic Challenges

Golf Taking Over:

- Family life revolves around golf
- Siblings feeling neglected
- Marriage stress
- Financial pressure

Rebalancing:

- Golf-free family days
- Sibling equity
- Couple time protected
- Budget reality check

Living Through Child:

- Parent identity tied to performance
- Emotional volatility
- Relationship strain
- Pressure multiplication

Healthy Separation:

- Your dreams vs. theirs
- Unconditional love reinforced
- Find your own hobbies
- Professional help if needed

THE MONTHLY PROBLEM-SOLVING SYSTEM

Week 1: Problem Identification

- What's the real issue?
- How long has it existed?
- What are the impacts?
- What's been tried?

Week 2: Solution Exploration

- Research options
- Consult trusted advisors
- Talk to other families
- Consider multiple approaches

Week 3: Implementation

- Choose approach
- Commit fully
- Monitor progress
- Stay flexible

Week 4: Evaluation

- What's working?
- What's not?
- What needs adjustment?
- Next steps?

CREATING YOUR CHALLENGE RESPONSE PLAN

Before Challenges:

1. Build strong foundation (joy, confidence, skills)
2. Develop family golf values
3. Create support network
4. Maintain perspective

During Challenges:

1. Stay calm and curious
2. Listen more than talk
3. Avoid quick fixes

4. Trust the process
5. Seek help when needed

After Challenges:

1. Reflect on lessons learned
2. Strengthen what worked
3. Adjust approach
4. Celebrate resilience
5. Build confidence for future

CHAPTER 11 ACTION ITEMS

This week, strengthen your challenge readiness:

1. **The Challenge Audit**: List current/past golf challenges. Note which solutions worked.
2. **The Support Network Map**: Identify three people you could call in a golf crisis. Reach out to strengthen connections.
3. **The Values Clarification**: Write your family's golf values. Post them visibly.
4. **The Prevention Plan**: Based on this chapter, what can you do now to prevent future challenges?

WHEN TO SEEK PROFESSIONAL HELP

Some challenges require outside support:

Mental Health Concerns:

- Persistent anxiety/depression
- Physical symptoms
- Sleep/appetite disruption
- Social withdrawal
- Academic impact

Family Dysfunction:

- Constant golf conflicts
- Relationship damage
- Communication breakdown
- Emotional volatility
- Lost perspective

Performance Issues:

- No improvement despite joy and effort
- Technical confusion
- Physical limitations
- Learning differences
- Specialized needs

SUCCESS STORIES FROM STRUGGLE

Maya's Comeback

Remember Maya who wanted to quit? Her parents implemented a complete reset:

- Two-month golf break
- Fun activities prioritized
- Pressure eliminated
- New approach designed together

Six months later, Maya was playing again—but differently. Shorter practices, games only, no score tracking, pure joy focus. She may never play college golf, but she'll play golf throughout her life.

The Plateau Breakthrough

Jake's eight-month plateau ended when his family stopped focusing on improvement. They played silly games, tried disc golf, and had putting contests with pool noodles. The pressure release allowed natural development to resume. His breakthrough came when he wasn't trying.

The Johnson Family Recovery

When golf nearly tore their family apart (daughter wanting to quit, son burned out, parents fighting), they instituted "Golf-Free February." That month saved their family and their children's love of golf. They returned with new rules: family first, golf second, joy always.

THE CHALLENGE REFRAME

What if we viewed challenges not as problems to avoid but as:

- Opportunities for growth
- Chances to strengthen bonds
- Teachers of resilience
- Builders of character
- Definers of values

Every family who navigates challenges successfully tells the same story: "It was hard, but it brought us closer and taught us what really matters."

YOUR CHALLENGE PREPAREDNESS

Challenges will come. The question isn't if, but when and how you'll respond.

Will you:

- Panic or stay calm?
- Force solutions or explore options?

- Protect your agenda or your child's joy?
- Go it alone or seek support?
- See failure or opportunity?

TOMORROW'S RESILIENCE BUILDING

Don't wait for challenges to arise. Build resilience daily through:

- Open communication
- Regular check-ins
- Joy monitoring
- Pressure awareness
- Perspective maintenance

Ask your child tonight: "How's golf feeling lately?" Then listen. Really listen. Without an agenda, without fixing, without judgment.

Because the families who thrive through challenges aren't the ones who avoid them—they're the ones who face them together, learn from them, and emerge stronger.

Your child's golf journey won't be perfect. It will have ups and downs, triumphs and tears, breakthroughs and breakdowns. That's not a flaw in the journey—that's the journey itself.

And how you navigate it together will matter far more than any trophy ever could.

What challenge will you transform into an opportunity?

CHAPTER 12

Maintaining Long-Term Motivation

The photo album told a familiar story. Page one: six-year-old Ashley beaming with her first junior clubs, eyes sparkling with possibility. Page five: nine-year-old Ashley holding a trophy, still smiling but something had shifted in her eyes. Page eight: eleven-year-old Ashley at practice, shoulders slumped, going through the motions. The final page was empty—by age twelve, Ashley had quit golf entirely.

"She loved it so much at the beginning," her mother reflected sadly. "I don't understand what happened. We supported her completely, got the best instructors, and never missed a practice. Where did her passion go?"

In another home, fourteen-year-old Marcus was packing his golf bag for the weekend. Not because anyone told him to, but because he couldn't wait to try the new shot he'd been imagining all week. Eight years into his golf journey, his enthusiasm had only grown. "Mom, can we leave early? I want extra time to practice my new rainbow wedge shot!"

Two talented young golfers. Two supportive families. Two completely different trajectories.

This chapter reveals the secrets of maintaining motivation across the years—not the fleeting motivation that comes from trophies or praise, but the deep, sustainable drive that creates lifelong golfers who play for the pure joy of it.

UNDERSTANDING MOTIVATION IN YOUNG GOLFERS

Motivation isn't a single force—it's a complex interplay of factors that evolve as children develop. What motivates a six year old (fun and parental approval) differs vastly from what drives a 16-year-old (mastery and peer respect).

The Two Types of Motivation:

Extrinsic Motivation (from outside)

- Trophies and awards
- Parental approval
- Peer recognition
- College scholarships
- Social media likes

Intrinsic Motivation (from within)

- Joy of improvement
- Love of challenge
- Satisfaction of mastery
- Connection with friends
- Personal accomplishment

Research consistently shows that while extrinsic motivation can spark initial interest, only intrinsic motivation sustains long-term engagement. The tragedy in junior golf? We systematically replace intrinsic motivation with extrinsic motivation, then wonder why children burn out.

THE MOTIVATION LIFECYCLE

Understanding how motivation naturally evolves helps you support it appropriately:

Ages 5-7: Pure Joy Phase

- Motivation: Fun and novelty
- Drivers: Play, exploration, parent time
- Threats: Pressure, boredom, criticism
- Support: Maximum variety, constant celebration

Ages 8-10: Discovery Phase

- Motivation: Competence and friendship
- Drivers: Skill development, social play
- Threats: Comparison, repetition
- Support: Peer connections, diverse challenges

Ages 11-13: Identity Phase

- Motivation: Belonging and recognition
- Drivers: Team inclusion, personal style
- Threats: Social rejection, forced conformity
- Support: Autonomy, unique path validation

Ages 14-16: Mastery Phase

- Motivation: Excellence and future vision
- Drivers: Personal goals, competitive success
- Threats: Plateau, life balance
- Support: Ownership, resource provision

Ages 17+: Integration Phase

- Motivation: Lifelong relationship
- Drivers: Self-defined success
- Threats: Other life priorities
- Support: Flexible engagement

THE MOTIVATION KILLERS

Before building motivation, we must stop destroying it:

1. The Trophy Trap

When success is defined by hardware:

- Internal satisfaction disappears
- Comparison becomes constant
- Failure feels catastrophic
- Joy depends on winning

The Fix: Celebrate process achievements—courage shown, problems solved, effort given, progress made.

2. The Perfection Prison

When mistakes become failures:

- Risk-taking stops
- Creativity dies
- Anxiety builds
- Improvement stalls

The Fix: Make mistakes normal, even celebrated. Share your own failures. Focus on learning.

3. The Comparison Curse

When worth is relative to others:

- Unique journey lost
- Self-doubt grows
- Jealousy develops
- Motivation becomes fragile

The Fix: Ban comparisons completely. Track personal progress only. Celebrate individual style.

4. The Pressure Cooker

When stakes constantly rise:

- Fun evaporates
- Stress dominates
- Burnout risk increases
- Quitting is tempting as a relief

The Fix: Regular pressure breaks. Fun-only periods. Perspective maintenance.

5. The Boredom Bomb

When practice becomes routine:

- Engagement drops
- Progress slows
- Excuses multiply
- Passion fades

The Fix: Constant variety. New challenges. Creative freedom. Child-led exploration.

BUILDING SUSTAINABLE MOTIVATION

The Autonomy Accelerator

Nothing builds motivation like ownership. Progressive autonomy by age:

Ages 5-8:

- Choose between two games
- Pick practice music
- Design one drill
- Select targets

Ages 9-11:

- Plan practice segments
- Set weekly goals
- Choose competition schedule
- Create new games

Ages 12-14:

- Design full practices
- Manage equipment
- Select instructors
- Lead warm-ups

Ages 15+:

- Complete ownership
- Parent as consultant
- Self-direct all aspects of golf
- Teaching others

The Mastery Map

Children need to see progress to stay motivated:

Visual Progress Tracking:

- Skill trees showing development
- Video progress compilations
- Personal record boards
- Achievement collections

Milestone Celebrations:

- First-time achievements
- Personal bests
- Breakthrough moments
- Courage displays

The "I Did It!" List:

Document monthly:

- New shots mastered
- Challenges overcome
- Fears conquered
- Goals achieved

The Connection Creator

Relationships sustain motivation when individual drive lags:

Golf Friendships:

- Regular practice partners
- Tournament buddies
- Mixed-age mentorship
- Team experiences

Family Bonds:

- Parent-child rounds
- Sibling competitions
- Extended family events
- Golf vacations

Community Building:

- Local junior programs
- Charity events
- Teaching younger kids
- Golf service projects

AGE-SPECIFIC MOTIVATION STRATEGIES

Keeping Young Ones Engaged (5-8)

Daily Wins:

- "What was fun today?"
- Sticker charts for effort
- Silly celebrations
- Story creation

Variety Rules:

- New game every session
- Different locations
- Costume golf days
- Theme practices

Parent Participation:

- Play together often
- Be silly too
- Match their energy
- Show your joy

Middle Years Momentum (9-12)

Competence Building:

- Skill challenges with friends
- Personal record tracking
- YouTube trick shots
- Course management games

Social Integration:

- Team competitions
- Practice groups
- Golf sleepovers
- Peer teaching

Creative Freedom:

- Design practice days
- Invent new games
- Create shot names
- Build challenges

Teen Motivation Maintenance (13-17)

Goal Ownership:

- They set all goals
- Parent supports only
- Regular revision okay
- Process focus

Future Connection:

- College golf exploration
- Career possibilities
- Lifelong vision
- Current relevance

Leadership Opportunities:

- Mentor younger players
- Run clinics
- Volunteer at tournaments
- Assist with programs

THE MOTIVATION RECOVERY PLAN

When motivation wanes (and it will), implement this recovery sequence:

Week 1: Diagnosis

- What specifically has changed?
- When did it start?
- What else is happening in life?
- Listen without fixing

Week 2: Pressure Release

- Cancel non-essential golf
- Return to pure fun
- Remove all expectations
- Reconnect personally

Week 3: Exploration

- "What would make golf fun again?"
- Try completely different formats
- Explore other interests too
- Give space and time

Week 4: Rebuilding

- Implement their ideas
- Start small
- Celebrate any engagement
- Follow their lead

CREATING MOTIVATION RITUALS

Pre-Practice Primers:

- Special music playlist
- Goal setting together
- Energy snacks
- Excitement building

During-Practice Motivators:

- Achievement announcements
- Progress recognition
- Energy management
- Celebration breaks

Post-Practice Reinforcement:

- Highlight reel discussion
- Progress documentation
- Next time planning
- Gratitude expression

THE LONG-TERM VIEW

Remember: Motivation isn't linear.

Expect and plan for:

Natural Fluctuations:

- Seasonal variations
- Life event impacts
- Development stages
- Interest cycles

Healthy Breaks:

- Other sport seasons
- Family priorities
- Academic demands
- Social needs

Evolution Not Extinction:

- Competitive to recreational
- Individual to social
- Intense to casual
- Active to passive

CHAPTER 12 ACTION ITEMS

This week, fuel sustainable motivation:

1. **The Motivation Assessment**: Rate your child's current motivation (1-10). Identify what's working and what's not.
2. **The Autonomy Audit**: List 5 decisions your child could start making for themselves about golf. Implement this week.
3. **The Connection Plan**: Identify 1 new way to build golf relationships (friend, mentor, group).
4. **The Joy Check**: Ask your child to list their 3 favorite things about golf. Build from there.

WARNING SIGNS OF MOTIVATION CRISIS

Watch for these indicators:

Behavioral Changes:

- Making excuses to skip
- Going through the motions
- No practice requests
- Lost enthusiasm

Emotional Indicators:

- Golf becomes "work"
- Resentment is building
- Joy completely absent
- Relief when they get a break

Physical Signs:

- Mystery illnesses
- Fatigue increasing
- Performance dropping
- Energy depleted

Social Shifts:

- Avoiding golf friends
- Hiding golf identity
- Embarrassment about playing
- Isolation is increasing

SUCCESS STORIES IN SUSTAINED MOTIVATION

The Chen Family Method

The Chens noticed their daughter's motivation dropping at age 11. Instead of pushing harder, they:

- Let her take a two-month break
- Restarted with friend-focused golf
- Eliminated all score tracking
- Made practice completely optional

Result: She chose to practice more than ever and still plays enthusiastically at 16.

Marcus's Magic

Remember Marcus? His secret:

- Parents never mentioned scores
- Practice always included creation time

- He taught younger kids monthly
- Connected golf to video game interests

Eight years in, he plays more for love than ever.

THE MOTIVATION PHILOSOPHY

Adopt these beliefs for long-term success:

1. **Motivation is cultivated, not demanded**
2. **Intrinsic always beats extrinsic**
3. **Autonomy accelerates engagement**
4. **Relationships sustain engagement**
5. **Breaks prevent breakdowns**
6. **Evolution is natural and healthy**
7. **Joy is the ultimate fuel**

YOUR DAILY MOTIVATION MISSION

Tomorrow, commit to:

- Finding one thing to genuinely praise
- Giving one new choice to your child
- Creating one moment of pure fun
- Connecting golf to their interests
- Celebrating progress, not perfection

THE ULTIMATE TRUTH

Children don't lose motivation—they lose connection to what motivated them initially. Your job isn't to motivate your child. It's to:

- Protect their natural motivation
- Remove motivation killers

- Provide motivation fuel
- Support motivation evolution
- Trust their motivation wisdom

Heren's an update on Ashley, whose story opened this chapter. Her parents took this information to heart and made dramatic changes. They stopped tracking scores, started playing fun rounds as a family, connected her with creative golf friends, and gave her complete control over her practice. Two years later, she's playing again—differently, but joyfully.

Because motivation isn't about pushing harder when passion fades. It's about understanding why it faded and creating conditions where it naturally regenerates.

Your child started golf with pure motivation—the simple joy of hitting a ball and watching it fly. Everything else is either fuel for that fire or water on it.

Which will you provide tomorrow?

PART IV

CREATING A SUSTAINABLE JOURNEY

CHAPTER 13

Balancing Golf with Childhood

The email arrived from the elite junior golf academy with the subject line every golf parent supposedly dreams of seeing: "Congratulations! Your child has been accepted into our Champions Program." The requirements were staggering: five days a week of practice, weekend tournaments, summer intensives, fitness training, mental coaching, and a "suggested" homeschooling program to accommodate the schedule.

Ten-year-old Sophia's dad, Mike, stared at the screen. This was what they'd worked toward, wasn't it? The fast track to college golf, maybe even professional? But as he watched Sophia through the window, building a fort with her best friend, both girls laughing hysterically, a different question emerged: At what cost?

Across town, twelve-year-old James was living a different reality. Despite obvious talent and love for golf, his family had made a radical decision: golf would enhance his childhood, not replace it. He played soccer in fall, snowboarded in winter, and golfed in spring and summer. He attended every school dance, went to summer camp with non-golf friends, and had regular kid adventures. His golf ranking? Lower than peers who specialized. His joy in life and golf? Off the charts.

Two paths diverged in youth golf. This chapter helps you choose the one that leads to both golf success AND a rich, full childhood—because they're not mutually exclusive, despite what the golf industry might tell you.

THE CHILDHOOD ROBBERY IN YOUTH SPORTS

We're living through an epidemic of professionalized childhood. Kids as young as eight have schedules that would exhaust CEOs. The average committed junior golfer:

- Practices 15-20 hours per week
- Misses family gatherings for tournaments
- Has few non-golf friends
- Defines identity through golf performance
- Experiences adult-level pressure

What's been lost? Only everything that makes childhood magical:

- Unstructured play time
- Diverse friendships
- Family traditions
- Academic exploration
- Other interests
- The right to be a kid

THE MULTI-SPORT ADVANTAGE

Despite pressure to specialize early, research is unequivocal:

Multi-sport athletes:

- Have 50 percent fewer overuse injuries
- Display better overall athleticism
- Show superior problem-solving skills

- Maintain motivation longer
- Achieve higher elite performance rates
- Enjoy sports into adulthood

Early specializers:

- Burn out by early teens (70 percent quit)
- Suffer more injuries
- Have limited movement patterns
- Lose intrinsic motivation
- Struggle with identity beyond sport
- Rarely play as adults

Sports That Complement Golf:

Baseball/Softball

- Rotational power
- Hand-eye coordination
- Mental toughness
- Strategic thinking

Tennis

- Racquet awareness
- Individual competition
- Mental resilience
- Quick adjustments

Soccer

- Lower body strength
- Cardiovascular fitness
- Improved coachability
- Spatial awareness

Swimming

- Core strength
- Flexibility
- Individual training discipline
- Breath control

Martial Arts

- Balance and flexibility
- Mental discipline
- Respect and humility
- Mind-body connection

AGE-APPROPRIATE LIFE BALANCE

Ages 5-8: Childhood First, Golf Second

At this age, golf should be one small part of a rich childhood tapestry:

Recommended Schedule:

- Golf: 2-3 times per week maximum, 30-45 minutes
- Other sports: 2-3 different activities
- Free play: Daily, hours of it
- Family time: Meals, bedtime, weekends sacred

Non-Negotiables:

- Birthday parties over golf always
- School events prioritized
- Bedtime routine protected
- Play dates encouraged

Warning Signs of Imbalance:

- Child identifies only as "golfer"
- Missing normal kid activities

- Few non-golf friends
- Adult-like schedule

Ages 9-12: Expanding While Exploring

Interest may intensify, but balance remains crucial:

Recommended Schedule:

- Golf: 3-4 times per week, 45-75 minutes
- Other sports: At least one per season
- Academic clubs/interests: Encouraged
- Social time: Protected and prioritized

Key Principles:

- Seasons for different sports
- Breaks from golf are normal
- Friend variety important
- School comes first

Family Golf Rules:

- One golf-free day weekly
- Vacations include non-golf time
- Siblings get equal attention
- Dinner conversations diverse

Ages 13-16: Choosing with Wisdom

If specialization happens, it should be athlete-driven and balanced:

If Choosing Golf Focus:

- Still maintain one other activity
- Academic excellence non-negotiable
- Social life protected
- Regular breaks scheduled

Critical Questions:

- Whose dream is this?
- What's being sacrificed?
- Is joy still present?
- What's Plan B?

Balance Strategies:

- Off-season variety
- Cross-training activities
- Non-golf friendships maintained
- Life skills developed

Ages 17+: Preparing for Life

Whether pursuing college golf or not, life preparation matters:

Essential Development:

- Academic readiness
- Social skills
- Work experience
- Independence building
- Identity beyond golf

Reality Check:

- 99 percent won't play professionally
- Professional golf ends in college for most
- Life will continue for 50+ years beyond junior golf
- Childhood can't be reclaimed

PROTECTING FAMILY LIFE

Golf can enhance or destroy family dynamics:

The Family Meeting System

Monthly family meetings to assess balance:

Agenda Items:

1. How is everyone feeling?
2. What's working well?
3. What needs adjustment?
4. Upcoming conflicts to navigate?
5. Family goals beyond golf?

Rules:

- Everyone speaks
- All feelings valid
- Golf doesn't dominate
- Solutions collaborative

Sibling Equity

When one child plays competitive golf:

Equal Attention Strategies:

- Individual parent time scheduled
- Celebrate all achievements
- Activities for non-golfers
- Prevent resentment from building

Financial Fairness:

- Budget transparency
- Equal opportunity different forms
- Experiences over equipment
- Family activities funded first

Marriage Protection

Golf stress can strain marriages:

Protective Strategies:

- Weekly couple time
- Shared non-golf interests
- Financial agreement
- Parenting alignment

Warning Signs:

- All conversations about golf
- Disagreements over commitment
- Financial stress
- Lost couple identity

ACADEMIC INTEGRATION

Education creates options beyond golf:

Non-Negotiable Academic Standards:

- Homework before practice
- Grades determine golf participation
- School events prioritized
- All types of learning are valued equally

Using Golf to Enhance Academics:

- Physics through ball flight
- Math through statistics
- Writing through golf journals
- Geography through tournaments

College Preparation Beyond Golf:

- SAT/ACT preparation
- Leadership activities
- Community service
- Work experience

SOCIAL LIFE PRESERVATION

Friendships matter as much as forehands:

Maintaining Non-Golf Friends:

- School friends prioritized
- Birthday parties sacred
- Sleepovers scheduled
- Typical kid activities

Building Golf Friendships:

- Focus on fun, not competition
- Parents facilitate connections
- Group activities beyond golf
- Lasting bonds emphasized

Social Skills Development:

- Team sport experience
- Group project participation
- Conflict resolution
- Communication skills

THE CHILDHOOD PROTECTION PLAN

Create specific family policies:

The Non-Negotiables List:

- Family dinner nights
- One full day off weekly
- Family vacation annually
- School events attendance
- Bedtime consistency

The Flexibility Framework:

- Which events can be missed?
- When does golf take priority?
- How to resolve conflicts?
- Who makes decisions?

The Review Schedule:

- Weekly: Quick energy check
- Monthly: Family meeting
- Quarterly: Major assessment
- Annually: Full evaluation

CHAPTER 13 ACTION ITEMS

This week, recalibrate your family's balance:

1. **The Schedule Audit**: Map your child's weekly schedule. Calculate golf vs. other activities. Adjust if needed.
2. **The Childhood Checklist**: List 10 normal childhood experiences. Ensure your child isn't missing them.
3. **The Family Meeting**: Hold your first balance-focused family meeting. Encourage everyone to share honestly.
4. **The Protection Plan**: Create three non-negotiable family rules that protect childhood.

RED FLAGS OF LOST BALANCE

Child Indicators:

- Defines self only through golf
- No non-golf friends
- Misses major childhood milestones
- Adult-level stress
- Lost joy in other activities

Family Indicators:

- Everything revolves around golf
- Siblings feel neglected
- Marriage stress
- Financial strain
- No golf-free conversations

Life Indicators:

- Academic decline
- Social isolation
- Health issues
- Identity crisis
- Future anxiety

<u>SUCCESS STORIES IN BALANCE</u>

The Martinez Method

With three kids including one serious golfer, the Martinez family created "Fair Play Rules":

- Each child gets one special activity
- Family dinner four nights minimum
- Sundays are golf-optional
- Vacations rotate focus

Result: Their golfer still excels while siblings feel valued and family remains close.

James's Journey Remember James? By maintaining balance:

- Played three sports through age 14
- Kept straight-A grades
- Built diverse friend groups
- Developed multiple interests

At 16, he chose to focus on golf but brought superior athleticism, time management skills, and perspective. He earned a college scholarship and still loves the game at 22.

THE LONG-TERM PERSPECTIVE

Ask yourself: In 20 years, what will matter more?

- That extra tournament or family event?
- Perfect swing or confidence to try new things?
- Junior ranking or lasting friendships?
- Golf scholarship or being a well-rounded person?
- Early specialization or lifelong love of golf?

THE BALANCED CHILD ADVANTAGES

Children who maintain balance develop:

- Superior time management
- Diverse skill sets
- Resilience through variety
- Identity security
- Relationship skills
- Lifelong activity patterns
- Perspective on success
- Joy in multiple arenas

They also, paradoxically, often achieve more in golf because:

- Fresh perspective prevents burnout
- Cross-training prevents injury
- Life balance reduces pressure
- Multiple identities build confidence
- Diverse experiences enhance creativity

MAKING THE HARD CHOICES

Sometimes protecting childhood means:

- Saying no to "elite" programs
- Accepting lower rankings

- Missing some tournaments
- Choosing family over golf
- Prioritizing long-term health
- Trusting unconventional paths

These choices feel difficult when surrounded by specialized peers. Remember: You're raising a person who plays golf, not a golf-playing machine.

YOUR BALANCE COMMITMENT

Write and sign this commitment:

I commit to protecting my child's right to a full childhood. Golf will enhance their life, not consume it. When forced to choose, I will choose their long-term well-being over short-term golf success. I will ensure they develop as a complete human who happens to excel at golf, not a golf machine who missed their childhood. Their joy, health, and wholeness matter more than any trophy.

TOMORROW'S BALANCE CHECK

Look at tomorrow's schedule. Does it reflect a child's life or a professional athlete's? Are there moments for:

- Spontaneous play?
- Friend time?
- Family connection?
- Other interests?
- Simple joy?

If not, what can you change?

THE ULTIMATE TRUTH

The children who maintain balance don't just become better adults—they often become better golfers. They bring creativity from other sports, resilience from diverse challenges, perspective from full lives, and most importantly, a joy that survives because it's not their only source of identity.

Sophia's dad declined the elite academy invitation. Instead, they found a program that practiced three days a week, encouraged other sports, and valued childhood. Sophia still plays competitive golf, but she also plays violin, loves science club, and has sleepovers with friends.

At her last tournament, another parent asked, "How is she so relaxed out there?"

Her dad smiled. "Because win or lose, she knows she's going for ice cream with friends afterward. Golf is something she does, not everything she is."

That's the balance that creates not just great golfers, but great humans who happen to play golf.

What will you choose to protect tomorrow?

CHAPTER 14

The Competition Question

The conversation happens in every golf family, usually around age nine or ten. "Mom, Dad, I want to play in a real tournament!" The child's eyes shine with excitement and possibility. The parents exchange glances, knowing this moment represents a crossroads. Down one path lies the world of competitive junior golf—rankings, travel, pressure, and dreams. Down the other lies recreational golf—fun, family, and freedom.

But what if it didn't have to be so black and white?

Meet two families navigating competition differently:

The Johnsons dove headfirst into competitive golf when their daughter Emma showed talent at age eight. By age eleven, she was playing twenty tournaments a year, ranked in the state's top ten, and absolutely miserable. "I just wanted to see if I could win," she later reflected. "I didn't sign up for all this pressure."

The Parks took a different approach with their son David. They waited until he begged to compete at age ten, started with fun team events, gradually introduced individual competitions, and always kept one rule sacred: the moment it stops being fun, we reassess.

At fourteen, David plays about ten events a year, loves every minute, and consistently improves because he's playing for himself.

This chapter helps you navigate the complex world of junior golf competition—not with rigid rules about right and wrong, but with wisdom about what serves your unique child best.

UNDERSTANDING COMPETITION'S ROLE

Competition itself is neutral—neither inherently good nor bad. Like fire, it can warm or burn, depending on how it's managed. For some children, competition provides:

Positive Outcomes:

- Goal-setting opportunities
- Resilience building
- Performance under pressure
- Social connections
- Achievement satisfaction
- Life lesson laboratory

Potential Negatives:

- Anxiety and stress
- Identity through results
- Joy depletion
- Family strain
- Burnout risk
- Childhood loss

The key is understanding your child, your family values, and how to create a competitive experience that enhances rather than diminishes their love for golf.

READINESS INDICATORS

How do you know if your child is ready for competition? Look for these signs:

Child-Driven Indicators:

- Consistently asks to compete
- Shows curiosity about tournaments
- Handles practice setbacks well
- Enjoys playing with others
- Demonstrates emotional regulation

Skill Indicators:

- Can play 9 holes comfortably
- Knows basic rules and etiquette
- Shows consistent contact
- Manages frustration appropriately
- Displays good sportsmanship

Family Readiness:

- Parents are emotionally prepared
- Financial resources available
- Time commitment feasible
- Siblings' needs considered
- Support system in place

Red Flags to Wait:

- Parent more excited than child
- Significant anxiety present
- Perfectionist tendencies
- Emotional volatility
- Golf equals self-worth

TYPES OF COMPETITION

Not all competitions are created equal. Understanding options helps you choose appropriately:

Level 1: Social Competition

Characteristics:

- Team formats
- Fun atmosphere
- Modified rules
- Everyone celebrated
- Score secondary

Examples:

- Parent-child events
- Scramble tournaments
- Skills challenges
- Camp competitions
- Club junior days

Best For:

- First experiences
- Building confidence
- Social players
- Ages 6-10
- Fun is priority

Level 2: Developmental Competition

Characteristics:

- Individual and team mix
- Local travel only
- Appropriate divisions
- Learning focus
- Supportive environment

Examples:

- 9-hole events
- Local junior tours
- School golf teams
- Regional series
- Summer leagues

Best For:

- Skill development
- Regular competition
- Building resilience
- Ages 9-14
- Balanced approach

Level 3: Performance Competition

Characteristics:

- Individual stroke play
- State/regional level
- Rankings involved
- Travel required
- Serious atmosphere

Examples:

- State junior championships
- AJGA events
- National qualifiers
- Elite junior tours
- College showcases

Best For:

- Committed players
- College aspirations
- High skill level
- Ages 13+
- Competition lovers

CREATING HEALTHY COMPETITION EXPERIENCES

Pre-Tournament Preparation

Two Weeks Before:

- Discuss expectations (fun, learning, effort)
- Plan logistics together
- Practice tournament conditions
- Address any anxieties

Week Before:

- Normal practice routine
- Play practice round if possible
- Maintain regular life schedule
- Build excitement not pressure

Night Before:

- Early, quality sleep
- Normal evening routine
- Pack together calmly
- Positive visualization

Tournament Morning:

- Familiar breakfast
- Arrive with plenty of time
- Warm-up routine consistent
- Energy check-in

During Competition

Parent Guidelines:

- Stay calm regardless of scores
- Focus on effort and attitude

- Provide practical support (food, water)
- Avoid coaching or correcting
- Be present without hovering

Between Rounds Support:

- "How are you feeling?"
- "What's been fun so far?"
- "What do you need?"
- "I'm proud of you"
- (Not: "What did you shoot?")

Post-Tournament Processing

Immediately After:

- Celebrate participation first
- Food before golf talk
- Let them decompress
- Follow their lead
- Unconditional support

Same Evening:

- "What was your favorite part?"
- "What did you learn?"
- "How did you handle challenges?"
- "What made you proud?"

Few Days Later:

- Review together if desired
- Find growth areas
- Plan next steps
- Maintain perspective

AGE-APPROPRIATE COMPETITION GUIDELINES

Ages 6-8: Introduction Phase

- Maximum 4-6 events per year
- Team formats preferred
- 9 holes maximum
- Local only
- Fun-focused scoring

Ages 9-11: Exploration Phase

- 8-12 events per year
- Mix of formats
- Some individual play
- Regional travel okay
- Process goals

Ages 12-14: Development Phase

- 15-20 events reasonable
- Mostly individual play
- State-level competition
- Some overnight travel
- Ranking awareness okay

Ages 15-18: Specialization Phase (If Chosen)

- 20-30 events for committed players
- National level possible
- College recruiting considered
- Performance goals
- Still need breaks

MANAGING COMPETITION PRESSURE

Healthy Pressure Looks Like:

- Butterflies before starting
- Desire to do well

- Quick recovery from mistakes
- Learning from experience
- Maintained joy

Unhealthy Pressure Signs:

- Physical symptoms (nausea, headaches)
- Severe anxiety
- Fear of disappointing others
- Identity crisis with poor play
- Wanting to quit

Pressure Reduction Strategies:

- Focus on process goals
- Celebrate courage to compete
- Share your own failure stories
- Maintain life perspective
- Regular competition breaks

THE FINANCIAL REALITY

Competition costs add up quickly:

Typical Annual Expenses:

- Entry fees: $500-5,000
- Travel: $1,000-10,000
- Equipment: $500-2,000
- Coaching: $1,000-5,000
- Total: $3,000-22,000

Budget Management:

- Set annual limit
- Prioritize quality over quantity
- Share costs with other families
- Seek sponsorships/scholarships

- Remember: Money doesn't equal development

Cost-Benefit Analysis:

- What are we really buying?
- Is it sustainable long-term?
- What's being sacrificed?
- Are there alternatives?
- Is joy increasing with investment?

COMMON COMPETITION PITFALLS

Pitfall 1: Too Much Too Soon

- Playing up in age
- National events too early
- Every weekend scheduled
- Burnout by thirteen

Solution: Progress gradually, child-led pace

Pitfall 2: Results Obsession

- Checking rankings daily
- Mood tied to scores
- Comparison constant
- Process forgotten

Solution: Ban rankings, focus on growth

Pitfall 3: Family Strain

- Siblings neglected
- Marriage stressed
- Finances stretched
- Life imbalanced

Solution: Family first, golf second

Pitfall 4: Lost Childhood

- Missing school events
- No non-golf friends
- Adult pressure
- Joy depleted

Solution: Protect childhood fiercely

CHAPTER 14 ACTION ITEMS

This week, clarify your competition approach:

1. **The Readiness Assessment**: Honestly evaluate if your child (and family) is ready for competition using this chapter's indicators.
2. **The Values Declaration**: Write your family's competition values. What matters more than winning?
3. **The Season Plan**: If competing, map out a reasonable schedule. Include breaks and family time.
4. **The Budget Reality**: Calculate true costs. Have honest family discussion about sustainability.

ALTERNATIVE COMPETITION MODELS

The Season System:

- Spring: School golf team
- Summer: Individual events
- Fall: Other sports
- Winter: Golf break

The Monthly Maximum:

- One event per month
- Local focus
- Skills competitions included
- Family rounds count

The Goal-Based Approach:

- Three process goals per event
- Competition when goals need testing
- Break when goals achieved
- Child determines frequency

SUCCESS STORIES

The Williams Family Wisdom

After their son burned out at age 12 from over-competition, they created new rules:

- Maximum one event monthly
- Must play other sports
- No rankings discussed
- Fun rounds equal competitive ones

Result: He returned to competitive golf at age 15, refreshed and motivated, eventually earning a college scholarship while maintaining life balance.

Emma's Evolution Remember Emma from the introduction? Her family pulled back dramatically:

- Reduced to 10 events yearly
- Added team competitions
- Focused on friendships
- Celebrated courage over scores

She's now 16 years old, still competing by choice, heading to college (not for golf), and plans to play recreationally forever.

THE COMPETITION DECISION TREE

Ask yourself:

1. **Why compete?**
   - Child's desire → Proceed carefully
   - Parent's dream → Stop and reassess
2. **What type?**
   - Fun-focused → Green light
   - Results-obsessed → Yellow caution
3. **How much?**
   - Enhances life → Continue
   - Dominates life → Reduce
4. **At what cost?**
   - Sustainable → Maintain
   - Strain showing → Adjust
5. **Is joy growing?**
   - Yes → Right track
   - No → Immediate changes

YOUR COMPETITION PHILOSOPHY

Write your family's philosophy:

We believe competition should _____. We will always prioritize _____ over winning. We will compete when _____ and take breaks when _____. Success means _____, not just scores. We will reassess whenever _____.

THE ULTIMATE COMPETITION TRUTH

Competition is a tool, not a destination. Used wisely, it builds character, resilience, and joy. Used poorly, it destroys childhood, relationships, and love for the game.

The best competitors aren't always those who play the most tournaments. They're often those who compete with joy, maintain balance, own their journey, and see tournaments as fun challenges rather than identity tests.

Your child can experience the benefits of competition without sacrificing their childhood to it. The key is remembering that they're children first, golfers second, and your beloved child always—regardless of any scorecard.

Tomorrow, if your child asks about competing, you'll be ready. Not with rigid rules, but with wisdom about what serves them best. You'll know how to create competitive experiences that build rather than break, enhance rather than consume, and always—always—protect the joy that brought them to golf in the first place.

What kind of competitive journey will you choose together?

CHAPTER 15

Technology and Modern Golf

The scene at the junior golf clinic looked like a technology trade show. Eight-year-old Oliver stood frozen, staring at the launch monitor display showing his attack angle (-2.3°), club path (1.7° out-to-in), and face angle (0.8° open). His instructor pointed at the red numbers: "See? We need to fix these to optimize your ball flight."

Meanwhile, Oliver's friend Zoe was on the putting green with her grandfather, using a simple smartphone app that made dinosaur sounds when she made putts. "Listen, Grandpa! The T-Rex is happy!" she giggled, running to attempt another putt.

Two children. Two very different relationships with golf technology. One paralyzed by data, the other motivated by digital fun.

Welcome to modern junior golf, where technology promises to revolutionize learning but often complicates it instead. This chapter will help you navigate the digital landscape wisely—embracing tools that enhance your child's development while avoiding those that destroy feel, joy, and natural athleticism.

THE TECHNOLOGY EXPLOSION IN GOLF

Today's young golfers face an unprecedented array of technology:

- Launch monitors in every bay
- Swing analysis apps
- GPS watches
- Virtual coaching platforms
- Social media pressure
- Online instruction videos
- Biomechanical analysis
- Statistical tracking systems

The golf industry sells a seductive promise: more data equals better golf. But for developing young players, the reality is far more complex.

THE HIDDEN DANGERS OF GOLF TECHNOLOGY

Before exploring helpful uses, we must understand the risks:

Information Overload

Young brains can't process multiple data points effectively. When a child tries to improve attack angle, club path, face angle, and swing plane simultaneously, they become paralyzed. Their natural athleticism disappears under an analytical avalanche.

Feel Destruction

Technology emphasizes external measurement over internal feel. Children who rely on devices lose touch with their body's wisdom— the felt difference between solid and poor contact, the intuitive adjustments for different shots.

Comparison Culture

Social media and online platforms create constant comparison opportunities. Young golfers see peers' highlight reels, while forgetting everyone struggles. Self-worth becomes tied to digital metrics and online validation.

Position Obsession

Video analysis often focuses on positions rather than motion. Children develop mechanical, posed swings trying to match freeze-frames instead of flowing, athletic movements.

Joy Depletion

When practice becomes data analysis, fun evaporates. The simple pleasure of hitting balls transforms into a stressful examination of numbers and angles.

AGE-APPROPRIATE TECHNOLOGY GUIDELINES

Ages 5-8: Minimal and Magical

At this age, technology should be almost invisible:

Appropriate Uses:

- Fun sound apps for games
- Simple photo memories
- Basic distance markers (visual)
- Celebration videos

Avoid Completely:

- Swing analysis
- Launch monitors
- Technical measurements
- Position comparisons

Time Limits:

- Maximum 5 percent of practice time
- Never during actual swinging
- Only for fun and memories

Example Use: "The app plays music when you make putts!" NOT: "The app shows your putting stroke path."

Ages 9-12: Enhancement, Not Replacement

Technology can enhance but shouldn't dominate:

Appropriate Tools:

- Game-based practice apps
- Simple shot tracking
- Basic video for progress memories
- GPS for course strategy learning

Still Avoid:

- Complex swing analysis
- Multiple data points
- Constant measurement
- Social comparison

Guidelines:

- Maximum 10-15 percent of practice
- Focus on games and fun

- Child-controlled usage
- Results over positions

Example Use: "The app shows you hit it farther when you're relaxed!"
NOT: "Your swing plane is 3 degrees too flat."

Ages 13-16: Strategic Support

Older juniors can handle more, but wisdom is crucial:

Useful Applications:

- Performance tracking (patterns not positions)
- Video for major changes only
- Mental game apps
- Competition preparation tools

Proceed Cautiously:

- Launch monitor data (simplified)
- Online instruction (curated)
- Social media presence
- Equipment fitting technology

Balance Required:

- Technology sessions separate from play
- Feel practice remains primary
- Regular tech-free periods
- Joy monitoring is constant

Ages 17+: Mature Integration

Near-adults can use technology more extensively:

Full Access Appropriate:

- Comprehensive statistics
- 3D/Video analysis (with guidance)
- Training apps
- Recruiting platforms

Self-Regulation Skills:

- Knowing when to disconnect
- Maintaining feel priority
- Avoiding comparison traps
- Using data wisely

TECHNOLOGY THAT HELPS VS. HURTS

HELPFUL Technology

1. Game-Based Learning Apps

- Make practice fun
- Create variety
- Track progress playfully
- Build engagement

Examples: Apps with challenges, virtual competitions with friends, skill-building games

2. Simple Progress Tracking

- Shows improvement over time
- Focuses on outcomes not positions
- Celebrates personal bests
- Visual motivation

Examples: Shot tracking apps, digital scorecards, progress journals

3. Communication Tools

- Connect with coaches remotely
- Share achievements with family
- Build golf communities
- Schedule coordination

Examples: Team apps, video sharing for feedback, tournament planning tools

4. Educational Resources

- Rules learning
- Course management
- Mental game development
- Golf history/culture

Examples: Rules apps, strategy guides, mindfulness tools

HARMFUL Technology

1. Complex Analysis Systems

- Create paralysis
- Destroy natural motion
- Build position obsession
- Reduce athleticism

Examples: Multi-angle swing analyzers, biomechanical measurements

2. Constant Measurement

- Prevent feel development
- Create data dependency
- Interrupt flow
- Reduce joy

Examples: Every-shot launch monitors, continuous swing monitoring

3. Comparison Platforms

- Damage self-esteem
- Create unrealistic expectations
- Build anxiety
- Focus on others

Examples: Ranking obsession apps, social media highlight reels

4. Information Overload Systems

- Overwhelm young minds
- Create confusion
- Miss developmental readiness
- Complicate simple games

Examples: Apps with 50+ data points, complex statistical analysis

CREATING HEALTHY TECHNOLOGY HABITS

The Family Technology Agreement

Create clear guidelines together:

Screen Time Limits:

- Practice: Maximum 10 percent technology
- Home: Designated golf tech time
- Bedtime: No screens 1 hour before
- Family: Tech-free golf discussions

Usage Rules:

- Technology enhances, never replaces feel
- Fun and learning prioritized
- No comparisons to others
- Regular digital detoxes

Parent Modeling:

- Limited phone use during golf
- Focus on experience over documentation
- Celebrate without posting
- Presence over capturing photos and video

The Weekly Technology Rhythm

Monday: Tech-Free Monday

- Pure feel practice
- No measurements
- Game-based only
- Connection focus

Wednesday: Wonder Wednesday

- Explore one new tech tool
- Fun applications only
- Child leads exploration
- Joy measurement

Friday: Tracking Friday

- Progress documentation
- Week's highlights reviewed
- Achievements celebrated
- Plans made for next week

Weekend: Balanced Approach

- Minimal technology on course
- Experience over recording
- Real connections
- Memory making

SMART IMPLEMENTATION STRATEGIES

When technology truly helps, implement wisely:

The Introduction Protocol

Week 1: Observation

- Use technology to observe only
- No changes based on data
- Note patterns
- Build baseline

Week 2: Single Focus

- Choose ONE improvement area
- Use technology to support
- Keep it simple
- Celebrate progress

Week 3: Feel Integration

- Connect data to sensations
- "The monitor shows what you felt"
- Technology confirms feel
- Internal awareness is primary

Week 4: Sustainable Rhythm

- Regular but not constant
- Purpose-driven use

- Balance maintained
- Joy protected

CHAPTER 15 ACTION ITEMS

This week, optimize your technology approach:

1. **The Technology Audit**: List all golf technology currently used. Rate each: Helpful or Harmful?
2. **The Digital Detox**: Try one completely tech-free practice. Note differences in engagement and joy.
3. **The Family Agreement**: Create technology rules together. Post them visibly.
4. **The Feel Test**: After using any technology, ask: "Did this help you feel your swing better?"

RED FLAGS OF TECHNOLOGY OVERUSE

Watch for these warning signs:

Behavioral Changes:

- Constantly checking devices
- Anxiety without technology
- Refusing tech-free practice
- Numbers obsession

Performance Issues:

- Mechanical movements
- Lost athleticism
- Decreased feel
- Position paralysis

Emotional Indicators:

- Increased frustration
- Joy decrease
- Comparison anxiety
- Confidence erosion

Social Impact:

- Isolated practice
- Online over real relationships
- Validation seeking
- Presence problems

SUCCESS STORIES IN BALANCED TECHNOLOGY USE

The Martinez Method

After their daughter became paralyzed by swing analysis apps, the Martinez family instituted "Feel First Fridays"—no technology allowed. They discovered she played her best golf after tech-free sessions. Now they use video only monthly for major checks, focusing on feel daily.

Oliver's Transformation

Remember Oliver from the introduction? His parents removed all launch monitor access for three months, replacing it with game-based practice. His natural swing returned, his joy exploded, and ironically, when they finally checked the launch monitor again, all his numbers had improved without him trying.

TEACHING DIGITAL WISDOM

Help your child develop healthy technology relationships:

Critical Thinking Skills:

- "Does this help you play better?"
- "How does it make you feel?"
- "What matters more—numbers or fun?"
- "When is technology helpful?"

Self-Regulation Development:

- Choosing when to use tools
- Recognizing overuse
- Taking voluntary breaks
- Maintaining balance

Value Clarification:

- Experience over documentation
- Feel over measurement
- Joy over optimization
- Connection over posting

THE FUTURE OF JUNIOR GOLF TECHNOLOGY

As technology continues evolving, maintain these principles:

Timeless Truths:

- Feel matters most
- Joy indicates health
- Human connection is essential
- Childhood is precious
- Simple is often better

Evaluation Questions for New Technology:

1. Does it enhance feel or replace it?
2. Does it increase joy or create stress?
3. Does it support development or complicate it?
4. Does it connect people or isolate them?
5. Does it honor childhood or rush it?

YOUR TECHNOLOGY PHILOSOPHY

Complete this statement to create your family's philosophy on technology:

We believe technology should _____ our golf experience, not dominate it. We will use tools that _____ while avoiding those that _____. Our priority is always _____ over data. When in doubt, we choose _____ over digital solutions.

TOMORROW'S PRACTICE

Plan tomorrow's session with intentional technology use:

- What tools truly help your child?
- What could you eliminate?
- How can you prioritize feel?
- Where can you add more fun?

Consider starting with a completely tech-free practice, then mindfully adding only what genuinely enhances the experience.

THE ULTIMATE TECHNOLOGY TRUTH

Technology is a tool, not a requirement. In the right hands, used wisely, it can enhance learning and fun. Used carelessly, it can destroy the very essence of why children love golf—the simple joy of hitting a ball and watching it fly.

Your child doesn't need every technological advancement to become a great golfer.

They need:

- Freedom to develop feel
- Protection from overwhelm
- Tools that enhance joy
- Space for natural learning
- Technology as servant, not master

The children who thrive in modern golf aren't those with the most data. They're those who maintain their athletic instincts, trust their feel, and use technology wisely to support—never replace—their natural learning process.

Zoe, with her dinosaur putting app, understands something Oliver's instructor missed: technology should make golf more fun, not more complicated. When it does, learning accelerates. When it doesn't, we've lost our way.

What relationship with technology will you model tomorrow?

CHAPTER 16

Building Your Support Team

Lisa sat in her car outside the golf facility feeling overwhelmed. Her ten-year-old daughter Emma had just finished another lesson where the instructor spent forty-five minutes adjusting her grip while Emma's eyes glazed over. The other parents seemed to have it all figured out—talking about swing coaches, mental performance experts, fitness trainers, and tournament schedules. Lisa felt alone, confused, and wondered if she was failing her daughter.

Two miles away, the Chen family was having their weekly "Golf Team Meeting" at their favorite pizza place. Around the table sat not just parents and their twelve-year-old son Michael, but also his easy-going instructor Jake, two other junior golf families they'd befriended, and Michael's school teacher who'd become an informal mentor. They were laughing about Michael's creative shot attempts while planning the next month's practice games.

Two families. Two completely different support experiences. One struggling in isolation, one thriving in community.

This chapter reveals the secret successful junior golf families know: you can't do this alone, nor should you try. Building the right support team transforms the journey from overwhelming burden to shared adventure.

WHY SUPPORT TEAMS MATTER

Raising a young golfer involves challenges no parent can navigate solo. You can get help and support with common issues such as:

- Technical knowledge gaps
- Emotional roller coasters
- Time and logistics demands
- Financial pressures
- Competing advice
- Development questions
- Balance struggles

The right support team provides:

- Expertise without agenda
- Emotional stability
- Shared resources
- Different perspectives
- Collective wisdom
- Distributed pressure
- Community joy

THE ESSENTIAL TEAM MEMBERS

1. The Right Instructor/Coach

This is your most crucial team member. The right instructor:

Understands Child Development

- Speaks in kid-friendly language
- Prioritizes fun and discovery

- Adapts to learning styles
- Respects childhood needs

Shares Your Philosophy

- Values joy over positions
- Focuses on long-term development
- Maintains a healthy perspective
- Supports family balance

Communicates Effectively

- Regular parent updates
- Clear goal alignment
- Open to feedback
- Collaborative approach

Red Flags to Avoid:

- Promises quick fixes
- Focuses only on positions
- Ignores child's emotional state
- Resists parent input
- Creates dependence
- Prioritizes their agenda

Finding the Right Fit:

Questions to Ask:

- "How do you adapt teaching for different ages?"
- "What role should fun play in lessons?"
- "How do you handle frustrated children?"
- "What's your philosophy on competition?"
- "How do you involve parents?"

Trial Process:

- Observe a lesson before committing
- Start with single sessions
- Watch your child's response
- Trust your instincts
- Don't hesitate to make changes

2. Practice Partners and Golf Families

Other families navigating similar journeys provide invaluable support:

Benefits of Golf Friendships:

- Shared transportation
- Practice motivation
- Emotional support
- Resource sharing
- Perspective maintenance
- Celebration partners

Finding Compatible Families:

- Look for similar values
- Prioritize joy-focused families
- Avoid hypercompetitive dynamics
- Seek life balance
- Mix ages/stages

Building Community:

- Organize group practices
- Share meals after golf
- Create group chats
- Plan non-golf activities
- Support all children

3. The Mentor Figure

Every young golfer benefits from a mentor—someone who's walked this path:

Ideal Mentor Qualities:

- Older junior who loves golf
- Former junior maintaining perspective
- Adult who played as a child
- Non-parent trusted adult

Mentor Roles:

- Share experience
- Provide a different perspective
- Offer encouragement
- Model resilience
- Bridge parent-child gaps

Finding Mentors:

- High school golf teams
- Junior club programs
- Former juniors at facility
- Community connections
- Natural relationships

4. The Wellness Support

Physical and mental wellness professionals prevent problems:

Physical Support:

- Pediatric sports medicine doctor
- Physical therapist (golf knowledge)
- Flexibility/yoga instructor
- Nutrition guidance

Mental Support:

- Sports psychologist (if needed)
- School counselor awareness
- Mindfulness resources
- Stress management tools

Preventive Approach:

- Regular check-ins
- Early intervention
- Holistic health view
- Age-appropriate methods

5. The Reality Checkers

These people help maintain perspective:

Who They Are:

- Non-golf friends
- Extended family
- School teachers
- Other parents

Their Role:

- Remind about a carefree childhood
- Question golf priorities
- Celebrate non-golf achievements
- Provide balanced perspective

BUILDING YOUR SUPPORT NETWORK

Start Where You Are

Week 1: Assessment

- List current support
- Identify gaps
- Note stress points
- Define needs

Week 2: Exploration

- Visit different facilities
- Observe junior programs
- Talk to other parents
- Research instructors

Week 3: Connection

- Reach out to one family
- Try out a new instructor
- Join group activity
- Build slowly

Week 4: Evaluation

- What's working?
- What's missing?
- Next steps?
- Adjust approach

The Gradual Build

Don't try to build everything at once:

Year 1: Foundation

- Find right instructor
- Connect with 1-2 families
- Establish home support

Year 2: Expansion

- Add practice group
- Find mentor figure
- Build facility community

Year 3: Optimization

- Refine team members
- Add specialized support
- Create traditions

CREATING TEAM CULTURE

Your support team needs shared values:

The Team Charter

Create agreements about:

- Joy as priority
- Children's needs first
- Mutual support
- Respectful communication
- Shared resources
- Collective celebration

Regular Team Rhythms

Monthly Gatherings:

- Rotating host families
- Kids play, parents connect
- Share challenges/successes
- Plan upcoming events

Practice Groups:

- Weekly scheduled times
- Shared supervision
- Group games/challenges
- Social time included

Communication Channels:

- Group messaging app
- Important updates only
- Positive focus
- Resource sharing

MANAGING TEAM DYNAMICS

Common Challenges

Competition Between Children:

- Celebrate all improvements
- Avoid comparisons
- Focus on individual journeys
- Mix groups regularly

Parent Philosophical Differences:

- Respect diverse approaches
- Find common ground
- Set boundaries kindly
- Protect your values

Instructor Conflicts:

- Address directly and privately
- Seek understanding first
- Change if necessary
- Child's needs paramount

Time/Resource Imbalances:

- Contribute what you can
- Various contribution types
- Gratitude for all help
- Flexible arrangements

THE VIRTUAL SUPPORT NETWORK

Online communities can supplement local support:

Benefits:

- 24/7 availability
- Diverse perspectives
- Can ask questions anonymously
- Resource sharing
- Geographic independence

Healthy Online Engagement:

- Choose positive communities
- Limit time investment
- Verify advice carefully
- Maintain privacy
- Real relationships first

Warning Signs:

- Comparison culture
- Negative dynamics
- Overwhelming information
- Time drain
- Increase in stress

CHAPTER 16 ACTION ITEMS

This week, strengthen your support network:

1. **The Support Audit**: List current team members. Identify gaps using this chapter's categories.
2. **The Connection Challenge**: Reach out to one potential support person/family. Start simple.
3. **The Values Conversation**: Discuss what you need from support team with immediate family members.
4. **The Gratitude Practice**: Thank one current supporter. Acknowledge their contribution.

SUPPORT TEAM INVESTMENT

Building support requires investment:

Time Investment:

- Initial relationship building
- Ongoing communication
- Shared activities
- Mutual support

Emotional Investment:

- Vulnerability in asking
- Trust building
- Conflict navigation
- Celebration sharing

Financial Considerations:

- Shared costs possible
- Resource pooling
- Group discounts
- Creative solutions

Return on Investment:

- Reduced stress
- Shared joy
- Better outcomes
- Lifelong friendships
- Sustained journey

RED FLAGS IN SUPPORT RELATIONSHIPS

Watch for these warning signs:

Toxic Dynamics:

- Constant comparison
- Negative energy
- Drama creation
- Boundary violations
- Value conflicts

Unhealthy Dependencies:

- Overreliance on one person
- Avoiding direct parenting
- Financial exploitation
- Emotional manipulation

Misaligned Priorities:

- Winning over well-being
- Adult agendas
- Sacrificing childhood
- Joy depletion

When red flags appear:

- Address directly if possible
- Set clear boundaries
- Reduce involvement
- Protect your child
- Find alternatives

SUCCESS STORIES

The Village Approach

The Patel family felt isolated until they created "Sunday Golf Club"—rotating between four families for afternoon golf games followed by potluck dinners. Children played together, parents shared supervision, costs decreased, and everyone's joy multiplied. Three years later, these families vacation together.

The Mentor Magic

When eight year old Marcus struggled with competition nerves, his parents connected him with sixteen-year-old Sarah, who'd overcome similar challenges. Sarah's simple presence and encouragement transformed Marcus's experience. She taught him breathing techniques through games and shared her own struggle stories. Marcus now mentors younger players himself.

The Team Transformation

Remember Lisa from the introduction? She found two like-minded families and together they interviewed instructors until finding one who prioritized fun. They created a practice group, shared driving duties, and supported each other through challenges. Emma now loves golf again, and Lisa has lifelong friends who understand the journey.

BUILDING SUPPORT FOR DIFFERENT SITUATIONS

Single Parents:

- Network is especially crucial
- Share responsibilities
- Build chosen family
- Accept help graciously

Multiple Children:

- Coordinate with other families
- Sibling support systems
- Divide and conquer
- Equal attention strategies

Financial Constraints:

- Resource sharing is essential
- Group lessons/practice
- Equipment exchanges
- Creative solutions

Geographic Isolation:

- Virtual connections
- Periodic travel groups

- Local sport crossover
- Creative partnerships

YOUR SUPPORT TEAM COMMITMENT

Complete and sign this commitment statement:

I commit to building a support team that shares our values of _____. I will seek help when _____, offer support when _____, and always prioritize _____. I understand that accepting support is not weakness but wisdom, and that together we can create a better journey for all our children.

THE LONG-TERM VIEW

The support team you build today will positively impact life far beyond junior golf:

- Lifelong friendships formed
- Parenting wisdom gained
- Community values modeled
- Lasting network benefits
- Memories treasured forever

Children who see adults collaborating, supporting, and celebrating together learn more than golf—they learn how to build their own support networks for life.

TOMORROW'S TEAM BUILDING

Look at tomorrow's schedule. Is it a solo struggle or supported journey? Could you:

- Invite another family to practice?

- Share transportation?
- Ask for help with something?
- Offer support to someone?
- Express gratitude?

Start small. One connection. One conversation. One shared experience.

THE ULTIMATE TRUTH

The families who thrive in junior golf aren't those with the most resources or the most talented children. They're those who build villages along their journey—sharing struggles, multiplying joys, and remembering that golf is better together.

You don't need a perfect team. You need a real one—people who understand that raising a young golfer is about raising a human being who happens to play golf. People who celebrate effort over outcome, maintain perspective under pressure, and never forget that childhood matters more than championships.

Your team is out there. Start building it tomorrow. One conversation, one connection, one shared practice at a time.

Because when you have the right people around you, every challenge becomes manageable, every celebration sweeter, and the entire journey transforms from burden to blessing.

Who will you invite to join your team?

PART V

THE BIGGER PICTURE

CHAPTER 17

Life Lessons Through Golf

The college admissions essay prompt was simple: "Describe a challenge you've overcome and what it taught you." Seventeen-year-old Sarah smiled as she began typing. She could have written about academic achievements or volunteer work, but instead, she wrote about the day she four-putted from five feet in front of a hundred people.

She described the humiliation, the tears in the parking lot, and the choice she faced: quit or learn. She wrote about returning to that same green every day for a month, practicing short putts until they became automatic. But mostly, she wrote about what golf had taught her: failure isn't final, pressure is a privilege, and the only competitor that truly matters is who you were yesterday.

The admissions committee later said it was one of the most compelling essays they'd read. Not because of golf, but because of the character it revealed.

Ten years after writing that essay, Dr. Sarah Martinez saves lives as an emergency room physician. "Golf taught me everything I needed for this job," she reflects. "How to stay calm under pressure, recover from mistakes quickly, and trust my preparation when decisions matter. Every day in the ER, I use lessons learned on the golf course."

This chapter explores the profound life lessons golf offers young people—not as side effects of the game, but as its greatest gifts.

WHY GOLF IS LIFE'S PERFECT CLASSROOM

Golf uniquely combines elements that create powerful learning opportunities:

- Individual responsibility within social context
- Immediate consequences for decisions
- Self-officiating requires integrity
- Failure as constant companion
- Pressure in manageable doses
- Clear metrics for improvement
- Endless variety of challenges
- Mental and physical demands

Unlike many youth activities, golf mirrors life's realities while providing safe space to develop crucial skills.

THE SEVEN CORE LIFE LESSONS

1. Integrity When No One Is Watching

Golf is the only sport where players call penalties on themselves. This builds character like nothing else.

How It Develops:

- Counting every stroke honestly
- Overcoming temptation to improve lie
- Always playing by the rules
- Admitting mistakes publicly

Life Applications:

- Academic honesty
- Business ethics
- Relationship trust
- Personal accountability

Parent Reinforcement:

- Praise honesty over scores
- Share your integrity-building moments
- Discuss temptations openly
- Model ethical behavior

Story of Impact: Twelve-year-old Marcus called a penalty on himself in a tournament, costing him the win. The college recruiter watching was more impressed by his integrity than any score he could have achieved. Years later, as a business owner, Marcus credits that moment with shaping his ethical framework.

2. Resilience Through Inevitable Failure

In golf, failure isn't just possible—it's guaranteed. Even professionals fail more than they succeed.

How It Develops:

- Bad shots require immediate recovery
- Every round includes setbacks
- Perfection is impossible
- Progress isn't linear

Life Applications:

- Career setbacks
- Relationship challenges
- Academic struggles
- Personal disappointments

Building Resilience:

- Normalize mistakes
- Focus on response, not result
- Celebrate comebacks
- Share failure stories

The 18-Hole Metaphor: "Life, like golf, has 18 holes. One bad hole doesn't define your round, and one bad day doesn't define your life."

3. Emotional Regulation Under Pressure

Golf teaches emotional control in real-time, visible ways.

How It Develops:

- Managing frustration publicly
- Performing with audiences
- Handling unexpected situations
- Maintaining composure

Life Applications:

- Job interviews
- Public speaking
- Conflict resolution
- Crisis management

Teaching Moments:

- Breathing techniques
- Reset rituals
- Perspective practices
- Emotion acknowledgment

Real-World Transfer: Emma learned to manage her anger while golfing with breathing exercises. Now as a teacher, she uses the same techniques when facing challenging students. With these techniques for coping with anger and stress, she is able to maintain her calm composure which influences the dynamics of the entire classroom.

4. Patience and Long-Term Thinking

Golf improvement happens slowly, teaching delayed gratification in an instant-gratification world.

How It Develops:

- Skills take months/years
- Improvements in course management strategy
- Practice investments pay later
- Process over outcomes

Life Applications:

- Educational pursuits
- Career development
- Financial planning
- Relationship building

Cultivating Patience:

- Track long-term progress
- Celebrate small improvements
- Discuss investment mindset
- Model patience yourself

5. Decision-Making and Consequences

Every shot requires decisions with immediate, visible consequences.

How It Develops:

- Risk/reward evaluation
- Strategy formation
- Adaptation to conditions
- Learning from choices

Life Applications:

- Career choices
- Financial decisions
- Relationship navigation
- Daily problem-solving

Decision-Making Framework:

1. Assess situation honestly
2. Consider options/risks
3. Commit to choice fully
4. Accept consequences gracefully
5. Learn for next time

6. Social Skills and Etiquette

Golf provides structured social interaction across ages and backgrounds.

How It Develops:

- Playing with strangers
- Respecting others' space
- Following social norms
- Building relationships

Life Applications:

- Professional networking
- Cross-generational respect
- Cultural awareness
- Social confidence

Social Learning Opportunities:

- Playing with different groups
- Tournament interactions
- Club activities
- Volunteer events

7. Self-Reliance and Personal Responsibility

In golf, you can't blame teammates or rely on others to compensate for your performance.

How It Develops:

- Self-coaching between lessons
- Equipment responsibility
- Score accountability
- Personal practice

Life Applications:

- Independent work ethic
- Self-motivation
- Personal accountability
- Initiative taking

Building Independence:

- Progressive responsibility
- Decision ownership
- Natural consequences
- Supported autonomy

AGE-APPROPRIATE LIFE LESSON FOCUS

Ages 5-8: Foundation Values
- Taking turns
- Counting honestly
- Handling disappointment
- Trying again
- Being kind to others

Teaching Approach:

- Stories and examples
- Immediate application
- Simple language
- Consistent reinforcement

Ages 9-12: Character Building
- Integrity choices
- Emotional awareness
- Effort valuation
- Friendship skills
- Goal pursuit

Teaching Approach:

- Discussion prompts
- Real-world connections
- Peer examples
- Reflection time

Ages 13-16: Complex Applications
- Ethical dilemmas
- Pressure management
- Future planning
- Leadership development
- Identity formation

Teaching Approach:

- Socratic questioning
- Life parallels
- Mentor connections
- Independent thinking

Ages 17+: Life Integration
- Career preparation
- Relationship skills
- Adult responsibilities
- Lifelong habits
- Value systems

Teaching Approach:

- Partnership model
- Real-world application
- Future visioning
- Wisdom sharing

FACILITATING LIFE LESSONS

The Post-Round Debrief

Transform car rides home into learning laboratories:

Great Questions:

- "What did golf teach you today?"
- "When were you proud of yourself?"
- "What would you do differently?"
- "How did you handle frustration?"
- "What can we use from today in regular life?"

Poor Questions:

- "What did you shoot?"

- "Did you win?"
- "Why did you miss that putt?"
- "Who beat you?"

The Life Connection Moments

When life presents challenges, reference golf:

School Challenge: "Remember when you couldn't hit over water? You practiced until you could. This math is the same—we'll work through it."

Friend Conflict: "In golf, you show respect even when frustrated. How can we apply that here?"

Disappointment: "Bad rounds happen. Bad days happen. What matters is showing up tomorrow."

244 | BEYOND BIRDIES

CHAPTER 17 ACTION ITEMS

This week, make life connections explicit:

1. **The Lesson Log**: Document three life lessons your child learned through golf this week.
2. **The Connection Conversation**: Discuss how one golf skill applies to school/life.
3. **The Value Victory**: Notice when your child demonstrates a golf-learned value in daily life. Celebrate it.
4. **The Story Share**: Tell your child about a life lesson you learned through sports/activities.

BEYOND COMPETITION: SERVICE THROUGH GOLF

Help children apply golf lessons through service:

Junior Mentorship:

- Teaching younger players
- Patience development
- Leadership skills
- Empathy building

Community Service:

- Course clean up days
- Fundraising tournaments
- Equipment donation drives
- Accessibility assistance

Life Lesson Amplification: Service transforms personal lessons into community impact, deepening understanding and commitment to values.

THE TRANSFER TO ADULTHOOD

What Golf-Raised Adults Report:

Professional Life:

- Superior pressure management
- Ethical decision-making
- Resilience through setbacks
- Individual accountability
- Strategic thinking

Personal Life:

- Emotional regulation
- Long-term perspective
- Integrity habits
- Social confidence
- Healthy competition

Parenting:

- Teaching through experience
- Patience with development
- Celebrating effort
- Managing expectations
- Building resilience

LIFE LESSON WARNING SIGNS

Sometimes golf teaches children the wrong lessons:

Negative Patterns:

- Winning at all costs
- Building self-worth through scores
- Perfection obsession
- Excuse making
- Rule bending

Course Correction:

- Refocus on values
- Adjust environment
- Change influences
- Seek support
- Prioritize character

SUCCESS STORIES BEYOND GOLF

The CEO Foundation's Tech, Michael Chen credits junior golf with his leadership style: "I learned that blaming conditions doesn't change outcomes, supporting competitors creates better environments, and integrity matters more than quarterly earnings. Every board meeting, I draw on lessons from junior golf."

The Teacher's Patience Elementary Teacher Lisa Park: "Golf taught me that everyone learns at different paces, mistakes are necessary for growth, and staying calm helps others perform better. My classroom management style is basically my golf mental game applied to eight-year-olds."

The Doctor's Precision Surgeon Robert Thompson: "Golf taught me that preparation prevents poor performance, tiny adjustments create major changes, and you must commit fully to every decision. These lessons guide every surgery I perform."

CREATING YOUR FAMILY'S LIFE LESSON CULTURE

Regular Rituals:

- Weekly lesson sharing
- Golf-life connection discussions
- Value celebration moments
- Story collection

Visual Reminders:

- Life lesson wall
- Value statements posted
- Success stories displayed
- Display connection photos

Living Documentation:

- Lesson journal
- Video reflections
- Annual letters
- Legacy building

THE ULTIMATE LIFE LESSON

Perhaps golf's greatest lesson is this: You are not your score. Bad rounds don't make bad people. Good rounds don't create worth. You are valuable because of who you are, how you treat others, how you handle adversity, and how you keep showing up.

This lesson—learned through thousands of shots, hundreds of rounds, and countless struggles—creates adults who understand that life, like golf, is not about perfection. It's about persistence, integrity, kindness, and the courage to keep playing even when the course gets tough.

YOUR LIFE LESSON LEGACY

Years from now, your child won't remember every score or trophy. They will remember:

- How you helped them handle disappointment
- What you celebrated beyond results
- When you emphasized character over scores
- Why you taught them about perspective
- How golf made them better humans

TOMORROW'S TEACHING MOMENT

Golf will present a life lesson opportunity tomorrow. It always does. Will you:

- Notice it?
- Name it?
- Connect it to life?
- Celebrate its mastery?
- Build on it?

The scorecard measures performance. Life measures character. Golf develops both, but only character lasts.

What life lesson will golf teach your child tomorrow? More importantly, how will you help them recognize and embrace it?

Because in the end, raising a young golfer isn't about creating a champion. It's about using golf's unique classroom to develop a human being equipped for life's challenges, committed to its values, and capable of making their corner of the world a little better. That's the real victory. And it's available every single day on the golf course.

Chapter 18

Raising a Lifelong Champion

The photo album sat open on the kitchen table. David, now forty-two, flipped through its pages with his eight year old daughter Sophie beside him. "That's you, Daddy?" she asked, pointing to a picture of a gap-toothed six year old holding a plastic golf club.

"That's me," David smiled, turning the page. There he was at ten, laughing with his grandfather on the putting green. At fourteen, focused but relaxed during a tournament. At eighteen, teaching younger kids at a summer camp. His wedding photo showed him and his wife on a golf course at sunset. Pictures of business golf outings, charity tournaments, and father-son rounds filled the recent pages.

"You're smiling in all the golf pictures, Daddy," Sophie commented innocently.

David paused, realizing the profound truth in her observation. Through wins and losses, good rounds and bad, across nearly four decades, golf had been a constant source of joy in his life. Not because he'd become a professional—he hadn't. Not because he'd won championships—though he'd won some. But because his parents had given him golf as a gift, not a burden. As a journey, not a destination.

"Because Grandma and Grandpa made sure golf was always fun," he said. "Want to go hit some balls and feed the ducks at the course pond?"

Sophie bounced with excitement. "Can we play the putting game where we have to hit over the cups?"

Four generations. One gift passed down with wisdom and love.

This final chapter is about the ultimate goal—not raising a golfer, but raising a champion who carries golf joyfully through all of life's seasons.

THE TWO PATHS OF JUNIOR GOLF

Every family faces a choice, though it's rarely presented clearly:

Path 1: The Achievement Sprint

- Intensive early specialization
- Rankings and results focus
- Scholarship dreams driving decisions
- Childhood sacrificed for golf
- Burnout by late teens
- Golf abandoned in adulthood

Path 2: The Lifelong Journey

- Gradual skill development
- Joy and growth focus
- Multiple interests maintained
- Golf enhancing childhood
- Sustainable engagement
- Playing into their 80s

The tragedy? Many families choose Path 1 thinking it leads to Path 2. It rarely does.

WHAT LIFELONG GOLFERS SHARE

Research following junior golfers into adulthood reveals consistent patterns among those still playing at 40, 50, and beyond:

Their Junior Experience Included:

- Fun as the primary focus
- Variety in activities
- Supportive, not pressuring parents
- Friends met through golf
- Manageable competition
- Maintained life balance
- Positive coach relationships
- Celebrated small victories

Their Adult Relationship with Golf:

- Play for enjoyment
- Use golf for building and maintaining relationships
- Find peace on the course
- Share golf with their children
- Continuous learning mindset
- Gratitude for the game
- Life balance maintained
- Joy in simple moments

THE DEVELOPMENTAL LONG VIEW

Understanding the complete arc helps maintain perspective:

The Discovery Phase (Ages 4-8)

Goal: Fall in love with hitting balls **Success Looks Like:** Asking to play **Avoid:** Technical obsession, competition pressure **Plant Seeds of:** Joy, curiosity, connection

The Exploration Phase (Ages 9-11)

Goal: Develop skills through play **Success Looks Like:** Creative shot-making **Avoid:** Over-specialization, ranking focus **Plant Seeds of:** Resilience, friendship, growth mindset

The Decision Phase (Ages 12-14)

Goal: Own their golf journey **Success Looks Like:** Self-directed improvement **Avoid:** Living through them, burnout **Plant Seeds of:** Independence, perspective, lifelong vision

The Transition Phase (Ages 15-18)

Goal: Integrate golf into adult life **Success Looks Like:** Playing by choice **Avoid:** All-or-nothing thinking **Plant Seeds of:** Flexibility, adult friendships, new formats

The Sustaining Phase (Ages 18+)

Goal: Golf as lifelong companion **Success Looks Like:** Regular joyful play **Celebrate:** Sharing with next generation **Appreciation for:** The journey's gifts

BUILDING THE LIFELONG FOUNDATION

Joy Insurance Policies

Protect against future burnout:

Policy 1: The Fun Minimum

- Every practice includes play
- Laughter is mandatory
- Creativity is encouraged
- Mistakes are celebrated
- Progress is patient

Policy 2: The Balance Guarantee

- Other interests are protected
- Family time is sacred
- Academic priority is clear
- Friends beyond golf
- Childhood is honored

Policy 3: The Perspective Promise

- Character over scores
- Effort over outcomes
- Growth over rankings
- Relationships over results
- Journey over destination

Creating Golf Traditions

Traditions build emotional connections that last for decades:

Annual Rituals:

- First round of spring celebration
- Family club championship

- Birthday golf adventures
- Holiday putting contests
- End-of-season reflection

Milestone Markers:

- First birdie ball saved
- Course conquest map
- Hole-in-one fund started
- Age achievement rounds
- Generation connections

Memory Builders:

- Photo walls of joy
- Story collections
- Funny moment journal
- Victory variety (not just scores)
- Friendship chronicles

NAVIGATING THE DANGER ZONES

Certain periods threaten lifelong engagement:

The Early Teen Pressure Cooker (Ages 13-15)

Threats:

- Social comparison peaks
- Competition intensifies
- Identity questions emerge
- Other interests compete

Protection Strategies:

- Reaffirm multiple identities
- Celebrate unique journey
- Allow exploration breaks

- Maintain fun elements
- Connect with peers in positive ways

The College Transition (Ages 17-19)

Threats:

- All-or-nothing thinking
- Identity crisis post-junior golf
- Time constraints
- New priorities

Navigation Help:

- Frame as evolution not ending
- Find new playing formats
- Connect to local golf program
- Maintain home course ties
- Celebrate new phase

The Early Career Years (Ages 20+)

Threats:

- Lack of free time
- Financial priorities
- Geographic changes
- Life complexity

Sustaining Strategies:

- Flexible engagement
- Social golf focus
- Business connection tool
- Stress relief framing
- Simplified approach

SIGNS YOU'RE RAISING A LIFELONG GOLFER

Your child/teen shows these indicators:

Emotional Signs:

- Talks about "when I play with my kids"
- Creates golf games independently
- Shares golf excitedly with others
- Handles bad rounds with perspective
- Maintains joy despite struggles

Behavioral Signs:

- Practices by choice
- Teaches others naturally
- Seeks golf experiences
- Balances golf with life
- Returns after breaks refreshed

Relationship Signs:

- Has genuine golf friends
- Enjoys playing with you
- Respects all skill levels
- Shares the game generously
- Values connection over competition

CHAPTER 18 ACTION ITEMS

This week, plant lifelong seeds:

1. **The Future Vision**: Ask your child to imagine playing golf at age 40. What does it look like? Who are they playing with?
2. **The Tradition Start**: Create one new family golf tradition this month. Make it about connection, not competition.
3. **The Joy Audit**: List what brings your child the most golf joy. Commit to protecting these elements.
4. **The Legacy Letter**: Write a letter to your child about hopes for their lifelong golf journey. Save for future gift.

LETTERS FROM LIFELONG GOLFERS

From Sarah, 35, ER Physician: "Mom and Dad, thank you for never making golf feel like work. Those Saturday afternoons where we just played and laughed built my love for the game. Now, after brutal shifts, nine holes restore my sanity. Last week, I taught my daughter to putt using the same games you taught me. The circle continues."

From Marcus, 28, Teacher: "I nearly quit at age fourteen when everyone else was obsessing over rankings. You let me take a break, play basketball, and come back when ready. That saved golf for me. Now I coach the high school team, focusing on joy just like you did. Several parents have thanked me for giving their kids permission to just enjoy golf."

From Emma, 45, Executive: "The life lessons mattered more than any trophy. Integrity, resilience, patience—I use them daily. But mostly, I'm grateful for Saturday rounds with my teens now. Watching them discover what I discovered, supported by the same wisdom you showed. Three generations on the course together. That's the real prize."

YOUR LIFELONG LEGACY

Someday, your child will face their own parenting decisions. They won't remember your words, they will remember your actions:

- How you responded to bad rounds
- What made you smile at the course
- When you chose fun over practice
- Why you taught them to take a step back
- How you showed unconditional love

They'll either replicate the pressure or pass on the joy. Your daily choices write their future story.

THE FINAL SCORECARD

As you close this book, consider the only scorecard that matters:

In 30 Years, Will Your Child: □ Still play golf? □ Play the game with joy? □ Share golf with their children? □ Thank you for the gift? □ Have lifelong friends through golf? □ Use golf's lessons daily? □ Find peace on the course? □ Love the game?

If you can check these boxes, you've won everything that matters.

TOMORROW'S OPPORTUNITY

Tomorrow brings another chance to build toward lifelong love:

- Choose joy over perfection

- Select fun over grinding
- Pick connection over competition
- Favor growth over rankings
- Choose their happiness over your dreams

Small daily decisions compound into lifelong relationships with golf.

A CLOSING STORY

Remember David? His parents never pushed, never lived through him, never made golf his only identity. They simply shared something they loved with someone they loved more. They celebrated effort, handled disappointment with grace, and kept golf in perspective.

David never played professional golf. But he:

- Met his wife at a charity golf event
- Bonds with business partners on the course
- Patiently teaches his daughter
- Finds peace during life's storms
- Maintains friendships through regular games
- Serves on the junior golf board
- Gives back to the game that gave him so much

His trophy case is modest. His life is rich.

That's the goal. Not raising a golf champion, but raising a champion human who happens to play golf for life.

YOUR JOURNEY FORWARD

This book ends, but your journey continues. Every day brings opportunities to:

- Build joy
- Teach values
- Create memories
- Strengthen bonds
- Plant seeds
- Nurture growth
- Celebrate progress
- Love unconditionally

The game of golf is a gift. How you give it determines whether it is a blessing or a burden. Choose wisely. Choose joy. Choose the long view. Choose love.

Years from now, may your child look through their own photo album, smile at every picture, and prepare to pass on the gift to another generation—with wisdom, perspective, and boundless joy.

The first tee awaits. Not for perfect swings or low scores, but for another opportunity to share this beautiful game with someone you love.

Play on. With joy. For life.

CONCLUSION

Your Family's Golf Legacy

As you stand at this crossroads in your child's golf journey, you hold tremendous power. Not the power to create a champion—that's beyond any parent's control. But the power to shape how your child experiences golf, what they learn from it, and whether it becomes a lifelong source of joy or a burden from childhood they left behind.

Throughout this book, you've discovered:

- How children really learn (through play, not positions)
- Why joy accelerates development
- How to build confidence without pressure
- When competition helps and when it hurts
- What matters more than scores

But knowledge alone doesn't create change. Action does.

<u>YOUR THREE COMMITMENTS</u>

As you begin implementing these ideas, make three commitments:

1. To Your Child "I commit to supporting your golf journey without steering it. Your joy matters more than any score. Your childhood matters more than any ranking. You are loved for who you are, not how you play."

2. To Yourself "I commit to examining my motivations honestly. When I feel pressure rising, I'll pause and ask: Is this for them or for me? I'll celebrate my growth as a supportive parent as much as their growth as a player."

3. To the Game "I commit to protecting golf's gifts—integrity, resilience, patience, and joy. I'll model these values, celebrate them in my child, and ensure golf enhances rather than consumes our family life."

THE ROAD AHEAD

Some days will be easier than others. You'll face:

- Pressure from other parents
- Disappointment when progress stalls
- Temptation to compare
- Moments of doubt
- Challenge and struggle

In these moments, return to your why. Remember that you're not just raising a golfer. You're using golf to raise a human being who:

- Handles adversity with grace
- Celebrates others' success
- Finds joy in challenge
- Maintains perspective
- Values integrity
- Builds lasting relationships
- Continues learning
- Plays for life

START TOMORROW

Don't wait for the perfect moment. Start tomorrow with one small change:

- Ask about fun, not score
- Create a new practice game
- Share your own struggle story
- Celebrate effort over outcome
- Choose joy over perfection

Small changes compound into transformed journeys.

YOU'RE NOT ALONE

Thousands of families are choosing this path—prioritizing long-term love over short-term success, building whole humans over golf machines, protecting their kids' childhood while helping them develop life skills.

Find those families. Connect with them. Support each other. Share struggles and victories. Build communities that value what truly matters.

THE ULTIMATE SUCCESS

Twenty years from now, success won't be measured by college scholarships earned or tournaments won. It will be measured by:

- A phone call: "Dad, want to play nine?"
- A shared tradition continuing
- Life lessons applied daily
- Joy that survived adolescence
- Gratitude for the journey
- Another generation beginning

That's the success waiting for families who choose wisely.

YOUR LEGACY AWAITS

Every family's golf story is different, but the best ones share common themes: patience over pressure, joy over judgment, connection over competition, and love over results.

What story will your family write?

The pen is in your hand. The first page starts tomorrow.

Write it with wisdom. Write it with love. Write it for life.

APPENDICES

APPENDIX A

Quick Start Guide

DAY 1: THE FOUNDATION PROMISE

Before any clubs are swung or games are played, establish the foundation:

The Parent Promise (Read aloud to your child)

"Before we start this golf journey together, I need you to know something that will never change: I love you exactly the same whether you become a professional golfer or never play again. My love doesn't grow with birdies or shrink with bogeys. You are not your golf score. You are my child, and that's all you need to be to have all my love.

Golf is something you do, not who you are. We're going to have fun, learn, grow, and face challenges. Through it all, my love remains constant. That's my promise to you."

Sign here: _____ **Date:** _____

Post this where you'll both see it regularly.

Week 1: Assessment

- Complete Joy Audit (rate 1-10):
  - Practice enjoyment: ____
  - Course enjoyment: ____
  - Golf conversations: ____
  - Request frequency: ____
- Identify one pressure source to eliminate
- Plan one pure fun session

Week 2: Language Revolution

- Track internal vs. external focus
- Transform five common phrases
- Ask questions instead of giving instructions
- Celebrate discoveries, not positions

Week 3: Practice Transformation

- Replace one drill with a game
- Add variety to every session
- Include child in planning
- End wanting more

Week 4: Support Building

- Connect with one like-minded family
- Share struggles honestly
- Plan group practice
- Build community

Month 2 and Beyond

- Gradual implementation
- Regular family meetings
- Quarterly assessments
- Continuous adjustment

Appendix B

Age-Based Development Guide

Ages 5-6: Pure Discovery

- **Physical**: Basic coordination developing
- **Cognitive**: Concrete thinking, 5-minute focus
- **Emotional**: Immediate reactions
- **Golf Focus**: Fun only, contact celebration
- **Session Length**: 15-20 minutes
- **Competition**: None
- **Key Need**: Joy and exploration

Ages 7-8: Skill Emergence

- **Physical**: Improved coordination
- **Cognitive**: 10-minute focus is possible
- **Emotional**: Beginning self-awareness
- **Golf Focus**: Basic skills through games
- **Session Length**: 20-30 minutes
- **Competition**: Team/fun events only
- **Key Need**: Success experiences

Ages 9-10: The Golden Years

- **Physical**: Peak motor learning

- **Cognitive**: Pattern recognition strong
- **Emotional**: Peer awareness growing
- **Golf Focus**: Skill variety development
- **Session Length**: 30-45 minutes
- **Competition**: Local, fun-focused
- **Key Need**: Friend connections

Ages 11-12: Transition Time

- **Physical**: Growth spurts beginning
- **Cognitive**: Abstract thinking emerging
- **Emotional**: Identity questions
- **Golf Focus**: Maintain joy through changes
- **Session Length**: 45-60 minutes
- **Competition**: Moderate schedule
- **Key Need**: Patience and support

Ages 13-14: Identity Formation

- **Physical**: Major changes
- **Cognitive**: Complex thinking
- **Emotional**: Peer pressure peaks
- **Golf Focus**: Ownership building
- **Session Length**: 60-75 minutes
- **Competition**: Self-determined
- **Key Need**: Autonomy respect

Ages 15-16: Specialization Window

- **Physical**: Strength developing
- **Cognitive**: Adult-like processing
- **Emotional**: Future focus
- **Golf Focus**: Excellence pursuit (if chosen)
- **Session Length**: 75-90 minutes
- **Competition**: Performance level
- **Key Need**: Balance maintenance

Ages 17-18: Transition Preparation

- **Physical**: Near-adult capabilities
- **Cognitive**: Full development
- **Emotional**: Independence drive
- **Golf Focus**: Lifelong vision
- **Session Length**: Self-directed
- **Competition**: Personal choice
- **Key Need**: Future planning

APPENDIX C

Resources and Support

Finding the Right Instructor

Questions to Ask:

1. What's your teaching philosophy for juniors?
2. How do you make lessons fun?
3. How do you adapt to different ages?
4. What role should parents play?
5. How do you handle frustrated children?

Green Flags:

- Emphasizes fun and discovery
- Adapts to child's needs
- Welcomes parent involvement
- Focuses on long-term development
- Creates joyful environment

Red Flags:

- Position obsession
- One-size-fits-all approach
- Promises quick fixes

- Excludes parents
- Creates pressure

Building Your Support Network

Local Resources:

- Junior golf programs
- First Tee chapters
- PGA Family Golf
- Community centers
- School programs

Online Communities:

- Positive youth sports forums
- Parent support groups
- Development-focused sites
- Research-based resources

Key Organizations:

- Positive Coaching Alliance
- National Alliance for Youth Sports
- Aspen Institute's Project Play
- Youth Sports Research Council

Recommended Reading

Child Development:

- *The Power of Showing Up* by Siegel and Bryson
- *Mindset* by Carol Dweck
- *Drive* by Daniel Pink
- *The Talent Code* by Daniel Coyle

Sports Psychology:

- *The Inner Game of Tennis* by Timothy Gallwey
- *Golf Is Not a Game of Perfect* by Bob Rotella

- *Positive Pushing* by Jim Taylor

Youth Sports:

- *Changing the Game* by John O'Sullivan
- *The Matheny Manifesto* by Mike Matheny
- *Until It Hurts* by Mark Hyman

APPENDIX D

Troubleshooting Guide

"MY CHILD APOLOGIZES FOR BAD SCORES"

This is a critical red flag that they feel your love is conditional.

Immediate Response:

1. Stop them mid-apology
2. "You NEVER need to apologize for a score"
3. "I love you exactly the same"
4. Physical affection
5. Change subject to non-golf topic

Long-Term Fix:

1. Examine your post-round behaviors
2. Eliminate ANY difference based on scores
3. Have the unconditional love conversation
4. Repeat message in different ways until it resonates and they believe it
5. Consider family counseling if pattern persists

Remember: If your child feels the need to apologize for their golf performance, you've accidentally created conditional love patterns. This requires immediate correction before permanent damage occurs.

Common Challenges and Solutions

"My child wants to quit"

1. Assess pressure levels
2. Take break if needed
3. Return to pure fun
4. Address root causes
5. Let them lead

"Progress has stalled"

1. Redefine "progress"
2. Add variety
3. Change environment
4. Celebrate other growth
5. Trust the process

"Other kids are 'better'"

1. Ban comparisons
2. Focus on individual journey
3. Find different peer group
4. Celebrate uniqueness
5. Maintain perspective

"Too much pressure"

1. Identify sources
2. Eliminate what you can
3. Build coping skills
4. Regular breaks
5. Joy first always

"Lost the fun"

1. Stop everything
2. Return to games
3. Remove all pressure
4. Follow their interests
5. Rebuild slowly

APPENDIX F

The Parent Promise Card

Print it out, complete and sign, then post this card where you'll see it daily:

MY UNCONDITIONAL LOVE PROMISE

I, _____, promise my child _____:

- My love will remain constant through every round of golf
- Bad scores will receive the same affection as good scores
- My mood will not change based on your performance
- You will come home to the same amount of love regardless of results
- Your worth to me has nothing to do with golf
- I will love WHO you are, not HOW you play
- This promise is forever and unbreakable

When I fail (and I might), I will:

- Apologize immediately
- Reaffirm my unconditional love
- Work to better align my actions with this promise
- Remember that you are watching and learning
- Golf will enhance our lives, not determine our love.

Signed: _____ Date: _____

Witnessed by: _____ Date: _____

REFERENCES AND SUGGESTED READING

RESEARCH FOUNDATIONS

Motor Learning and Development

Newell, K. M. (1986). Constraints on the development of coordination. *Motor Development in Children*, 34, 341-360.

Schmidt, R. A., & Lee, T. D. (2019). *Motor Learning and Performance* (6th ed.). Human Kinetics.
Wulf, G. (2013). Attentional focus and motor learning: A review of fifteen years. *International Review of Sport and Exercise Psychology*, 6(1), 77-104.

Child Development

Piaget, J. (1952). *The Origins of Intelligence in Children*. International Universities Press. 5. Vygotsky, L. S. (1978). *Mind in Society*. Harvard University Press. 6. Erikson, E. H. (1968). *Identity: Youth and Crisis*. Norton.

Youth Sports Research

Côté, J., & Fraser-Thomas, J. (2016). Youth involvement and positive development in sport. *Sport Psychology*, 34-45. 8. Bailey, R., et al. (2013). Physical activity: An underestimated investment in human capital? *Journal of Physical Activity and Health*, 10(3), 289-308.

Motivation and Psychology

Deci, E. L., & Ryan, R. M. (2000). Self-determination theory. *Psychological Inquiry*, 11(4), 227-268. 10. Dweck, C. S. (2006). *Mindset: The New Psychology of Success*. Random House.

Positive Youth Development

Fraser-Thomas, J., Côté, J., & Deakin, J. (2005). Youth sport programs: An avenue to foster positive youth development. *Physical Education & Sport Pedagogy*, 10(1), 19-40.

ADDITIONAL RESOURCES

Websites

- Positive Coaching Alliance: www.positivecoach.org
- Aspen Institute Project Play: www.aspenprojectplay.org
- TrueSport: www.truesport.org

Books for Parents

- *Until It Hurts* by Mark Hyman
- *Changing the Game* by John O'Sullivan
- *The Ride of a Lifetime* by John O'Sullivan
- *Home Team Advantage* by Brooke de Lench
- *Positive Sports Parenting* by Jim Thompson

Books for Young Golfers

- *The First Tee Life Skills Experience* Series
- *Golf for Kids* by SportKids Publishing
- *The Mental Game for Youth Athletes* by Dr. Patrick Cohn

ACKNOWLEDGMENTS

This book exists because of the countless families who shared their stories—both triumphs and struggles—with remarkable honesty and vulnerability.

Special thanks to:

- The young golfers who reminded me daily why joy matters most
- The parents who had the courage to change course when needed
- The coaches who prioritize development over winning
- The researchers whose work provides our foundation
- My family, for their patience during writing and wisdom throughout

To every parent reading this: Your willingness to examine and possibly change your approach takes tremendous courage. Your child is fortunate to have someone who cares enough to seek better ways.

May your journey be filled with more joy than you imagined possible.

A FINAL WORD

If you take only one message from this book, let it be this:

Your child's relationship with golf will mirror your relationship with their golf journey. Choose joy, and they will too. Choose pressure, and they will feel it. Choose love over results, and they will play with freedom.

The game of golf offers profound gifts—integrity, resilience, patience, and joy. But these gifts can only be received with open hands, not grasping ones.

Hold your child's golf journey lightly. Support without steering. Celebrate without comparing. Love without conditions.

Do this, and twenty years from now, you won't be looking at dusty trophies wondering where the time went. You'll be on the first tee with your adult child, sharing another round in a lifetime of rounds, grateful for every moment of the journey.

That's success. That's legacy. That's love. Play on.

ABOUT THE AUTHOR

Joe DiChiara – Father, Golf Coach, Educator, Junior Development Leader

Joe DiChiara is a world-renowned golf coach with over two decades of experience coaching golfers of all levels—from beginners to major champions on the PGA and LPGA Tours. Recognized for his cutting-edge approach that blends biomechanics, motor learning science, and performance technology, Joe has earned a reputation as one of the most innovative minds in modern golf instruction.

Beyond his work with elite players, Joe is deeply committed to developing the next generation of golfers. He has built and led nationally ranked junior golf programs, designed skill acquisition systems grounded in research, and mentored hundreds of young athletes through every stage of their golf journey. His programs emphasize not just swing mechanics, but also character development, competitive readiness, and long-term athletic growth.

Joe's impact on junior golf is matched by his leadership in golf education. He was the Co-Founder and Director of the International Preparatory Golf Academy in Bangkok, Thailand—now one of Asia's premier junior golf development programs. During his tenure, he coached and mentored numerous young athletes into U.S. college golf scholarships and guided two-time U.S. Women's Open Champion Yuka Saso.

Joe has also held executive positions as Director of Education with leading golf technology companies such as K-Motion, 4D Motion, and

Sportsbox AI, where he helped bring advanced motion capture tools to coaches and athletes worldwide.

Currently, Joe resides in Phoenix, Arizona, where he serves as the Founder and Director of his golf academy as well as his online coaching programs. Whether on the range, in the lab, or guiding juniors toward college scholarships, Joe's mission remains the same: to make golf improvement accessible, personal, and transformative.

Joe would love to hear your story and can be reached at:

Joe@joedichiaragolf.com

www.ingramcontent.com/pod-product-compliance
Lightning Source LLC
Chambersburg PA
CBHW062048270326

41931CB00013B/2989